IMPACT OF THE CASE MODEL OF IDENTITY THEFT TRAINING

ON INFLUENCING PREVENTION BEHAVIORS IN SENIOR CITIZENS

by

Lorenza A. Whitfield, Jr.

A Dissertation Submitted in Partial Fulfillment of the

Requirements for the Degree of

Doctor of Philosophy

University of Fairfax

2007

AuthorHouse™
1663 Liberty Drive
Bloomington, IN 47403
www.authorhouse.com
Phone: 1-800-839-8640

First published by AuthorHouse 12/02/2009

ISBN: 978-1-4490-5158-7 (sc)

Library of Congress Control Number: 2009912730

Printed in the United States of America
Bloomington, Indiana

This book is printed on acid-free paper.

IMPACT OF THE CASE MODEL OF IDENTITY THEFT TRAINING

ON INFLUENCING PREVENTION BEHAVIORS IN SENIOR CITIZENS

by

Lorenza A. Whitfield, Jr.

has been approved

2007

We hereby certify that this dissertation, submitted by Lorenza A. Whitfield, Jr., conforms to acceptable standards and is fully adequate in scope and quality to fulfill the dissertation requirements for the degree of Doctor of Philosophy.

APPROVED:

Christopher V. Feudo, D.Sc.
Chairperson of Dissertation Committee

Norma Fleischman, Ph.D.
Dissertation Committee Member

Janice M. Orcutt
Dissertation Committee Member

ACCEPTED AND SIGNED:

_____   _____
Christopher V. Feudo, D.Sc.   Date
Chairperson

_____   _____
Victor N. Berlin, Ph.D.   Date
Chief Academic Officer

University of Fairfax

2007

Abstract

Impact of the Case Model of Identity Theft Training

on Influencing Prevention Behaviors in Senior Citizens

by
Lorenza A. Whitfield, Jr.

2007

Identity theft is one of the fastest growing crimes in the United States, costing $52.6 billion in 2004 alone. Victims of identity theft suffer long-term and well-documented pain and suffering. This is particularly true for senior citizens who comprise the demographic group most frequently victimized by this crime.

A review of literature revealed that training has led to positive changes in the attitudes and behaviors of trainees. Although there has been limited research on the impact of training with respect to identity theft prevention strategies, previous work by McKenna and Miller examined the effectiveness of the Citizens Against Senior Exploitation (CASE) Training Model on the attitudes and behaviors of trainees with respect to identity theft prevention.

This study provided validity for McKenna and Miller's work and focused specifically on senior citizens, with the goal of helping to address the needs of the group most vulnerable to identity theft predators. Both a treatment group and a comparison group of senior citizens were utilized to examine the changes in their attitudes and

behaviors with respect to identity theft prevention.

The findings indicated that the CASE Training Program influenced the adoption

of identity theft prevention techniques by senior citizens.

Dedication

This dissertation is dedicated to my daughter, Brittany. May she grow in knowledge and become the next "Doctor" in the Whitfield family.

Acknowledgements

There are many individuals I would like to acknowledge for helping me to complete this dissertation. First and foremost, I would like to extend my most heartfelt gratitude to Dean Janice Orcutt who served on my dissertation committee. Her attentive mentoring conveyed to me her enthusiasm for research and teaching, which I will always remember. In addition, I appreciate the attention to detail provided by Dr. Norma Fleischman, whose help with the research design was invaluable. Thank you to Dr. Chris Feudo for his support and encouragement; I will always remember his motto: "Just finish it Lorenza!"

I would like to express my appreciation to Dr. Victor Berlin, whose vision helped me to finalize my research topic. Thanks also to Janice Berlin, who has been a "mother" throughout this dissertation process. I would also like to thank my friends and co-workers with whom I have spent countless hours discussing this research.

I would also like to express my gratitude to Heritage Baptist Church, St. Philips Episcopal Church, Mt. Pleasant Baptist Church, and Wingler House participants for their participation in this study. A special thank you goes to Kristin Riggins, the Maryland DA Office CASE representative, whose assistance in this research was critical to the completion of this study.

I am grateful for the support of my parents, Lorenza and Maude Whitfield, who instilled in me a love of knowledge and the discipline I needed to achieve my goals. I would also like to thank my girlfriend Danita Hill for her love and support.

Finally, my deepest thanks to my daughter, Brittany, whose caring, patience, and selflessness allowed me the time and energy to focus on completing my academic pursuits with her compelling phase, "My daddy can do anything," which was followed by, "Are you finished with school yet, daddy? This is taking forever!"

Table of Contents

List of Tables

List of Figures

Chapter 1

Rationale

1.1 Problem Statement

Identity theft is one of the fastest growing crimes in the United States (Allison, Schuck, & Lersch, 2005; Federal Trade Commission [FTC], 2005a; Identity Theft Resource Center [ITRC], 2005; Karia & Asari, 2001; Lease & Burke, 2000; United States Postal Service [USPS], 2005).

Identity theft and identity fraud are the two terms most commonly used to refer to crimes in which a person wrongfully obtains and uses another individual's personal data (including name, birth date, and/or social security number) in a manner involving deception or fraud, with the intent to defraud, usually for economic gain (Edwards, 2003; O'Neill, 2003; Walters & Jackson, 2003). Typically, the stolen information is used fraudulently to apply for credit, take over banking accounts, purchase real-estate or other property, and/or to commit other unlawful acts.

According to the Federal Trade Commission (FTC) (FTC, 2006a), the rate of consumer fraud and identity theft increased 52% between 2002 and 2004. During calendar year 2004, more than nine million Americans were victimized by identity theft. In the following year (FTC, 2005b), the FTC received over 685,000 complaints regarding consumer fraud, of which 37% were specifically related to identity theft (FTC, 2006a). The primary identity theft attack methods are: credit card fraud, telephone-marketing fraud, utility fraud, real-estate fraud, loan fraud, and government documents/benefits fraud (FTC, 2005a). The National and State Trends in Fraud and Identity Theft Report (FTC, 2006a) confirmed in 2006 that credit card fraud accounted for 26% of all fraud cases and identified it as the most frequent form of identity theft in the United States.

Two of the most common forms of identity theft are "true name fraud" and "account takeover fraud" (Benner, Givens, & Mierzwinski, 2000). True name fraud occurs when an individual's personal information is used to open a new account. Account takeover fraud involves gaining illegal access to an individual's existing account for the purpose of making fraudulent charges against the account. Identity theft is also used to facilitate other crimes—including money laundering, bankruptcy fraud, computer crimes, and acts of terrorism—by concealing the identity of the criminal while he/she accesses funds or privileges of the victim (FTC, 2003a).

Credit card theft is the most common form of identity theft in America (FTC, 2006b; Walters, 2004). The American Association of Retired People (AARP) reported that older Americans are the age group most frequently victimized by credit card theft (Walters, 2004). In 2005, 22% of the 239,277 identity theft cases reported to the FTC were reported by individuals, 50 or over. Of the complaints recorded with the FTC, 26% reported that their personal information was misused in credit card fraud, 18% reported phone or utility fraud, and 17% reported bank fraud (FTC, 2006a). In the FTC report of 2003, 23% of complainants, ranging in age from 50 to 64, reported that their information had been used to establish new credit, while 17% reported that their information was used to access existing credit accounts. The survey also indicated that 24% of complainants aged 65 and over reported that their information had been used to establish new credit, while 20% reported it was used to access existing credit (FTC, 2004b).

1.2 Extent of the Problem

The total cost of identity theft in the U.S. was $52.6 billion in 2004 (Javelin/Better Business Bureau, 2005). Although technology has provided new opportunities for identity thief, many criminals still obtain personal information through traditional channels such as pick-pocketing, stealing records or information from job sites, and pilfering discarded trash (FTC, 2000).

The Privacy & American Business survey in 2003 found that 49% of the 98 million adults in the U.S. feel that they do not know how to protect themselves against identity theft; in addition, 34% reported that someone obtained their credit card information or forged a credit card in their name, and used it to make purchases.

An estimated 27.3 million Americans were victims of identity theft between 1998 and 2003 (FTC, 2004b). A total of almost 10 million individuals were victims of identity theft in 2002. In 2002, identity theft losses to businesses and financial institutions totaled $47.6 billion and consumer victims reported $5 billion in out-of-pocket expenses. Seventy-three percent of respondents to a 2003 survey by the ITRC reported that new credit cards had been opened in their names, and 27% reported incidents of account takeover (ITRC, 2003).

1.3 Response to the Problem

To prevent or limit the impact of identity theft, consumers must adopt identity theft prevention or detection behaviors (Milne, 2003). According to O'Neill & Xiao (2004) and studies conducted by Milne (2003), one of the best ways to detect identity theft is to order a credit report. Additional research published by FTC (2005b) and the Privacy Rights Clearinghouse (2003) also came to the same conclusions. In fact, AARP recommends a strategy of ordering a credit report from each of the three major credit bureaus and staggering the requests every four months.

However, a recent study found that ordering a credit report was the least frequently performed identity theft reduction strategy. The most common reasons for not taking advantage of this valuable resource included: cost, lack of time or knowledge of the process of ordering the report (O'Neill & Xiao, 2004). As a result, many identity theft victims do not realize that their identity has been stolen until months, or even years, after a crime occurs. Both the United States Postal Service (USPS) and AARP have reported that credit card fraud sometimes continues for two or more years before victims even discover it.

1.4 Significance of Contribution to Knowledge

Currently, several programs exist to provide identity theft prevention training for senior citizens. Two such programs are the online training program provided by AARP and the seminar-based training program conducted by the Communities Against Senior Exploitation (CASE). However, there has been limited research on the impact of these programs on changing the attitudes and behaviors of senior citizens with respect to identity theft.

This dissertation research included an investigation of the impact of one these programs—the CASE Training Model—on the preventive attitudes and behaviors of senior citizens by building upon the work done by McKenna and Miller (2003), which examined the effectiveness of the CASE model for training providers and senior citizens. In addition, by measuring the changes in attitudes and behaviors, as a result of the CASE training, this study sought to extend the research conducted by O'Neill and Xiao (2004) which suggested that identity theft training would help to increase the use of preventive behaviors by consumers.

The research questions guiding this dissertation study were:

1. Is there a relationship between participation in CASE training and attitudes towards identity theft prevention?

2. Is there a relationship between participation in CASE training and the use of identity theft prevention behaviors?

3. Is there a relationship between participation in CASE training and the practice of ordering a credit report?

Chapter 2

Research Literature Review

This study investigated the impact of training on the attitudes and behaviors of senior citizens with respect to identity theft prevention. This review of literature explored the following areas: the government's role in identity theft prevention, the effects of identity theft on victims, and identity theft training programs for senior citizens.

2.1 The Government's Role in Identity Theft Prevention

Milne (2003) emphasized the importance of the government's role in reducing identity theft in his study of this emerging crime. He argued that prevention of this crime depends upon the collective actions of government, businesses, and consumers.

Milne developed a model known as the Institutional System for Minimizing Theft, which is depicted in Figure 1. This model assigned primary responsibility for preventing identity theft to the federal and state government because government:

1. has the power and the ability to pass criminal and civil legislation to fight and deter identity theft;

2. can create new laws that influence business policy by requiring better information handling practices; and

3. can educate consumers to protect their personal information.

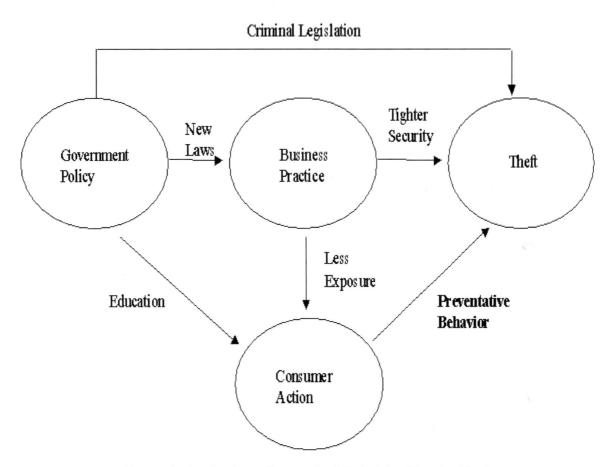

Figure 1: Institutional System for Minimizing Identity Theft

According to Milne (2003), actions by the government led to corporations adopting better business practices and limited consumer exposure. This ultimately caused a decrease in identity theft.

The Identity Theft and Assumption Deterrence Act of 1998 made the theft of personal information, with intent to commit an unlawful act, a federal crime in the U.S. Violators are subject to imprisonment for up to 15 years and a maximum fine of $250,000.

The Act identified an offender as:

" Anyone who knowingly transfers or uses without lawful authority, any name or number that may be used -- alone or in conjunction with any other information -- to identify a specific individual with the intent to commit, aid or abet any violation of federal law or a felony under any applicable state or local law" (S. Rep. No. 105-274, 1998).

This 1998 Act defined the crime of "identity theft" and prescribed penalties for violations, but did not address methods of prevention. However, prevention measures were adopted with the 2003 passing of the Fair and Accurate Credit Transactions Act (FACTA) (S. Rep. No. 108-159, 2003). The goals of the FACTA legislation were to reduce identity theft, to help victims recover, and to protect consumers by allowing free access to their credit histories. The major provisions of this legislation which are relevant to this study were as follows:

1. A requirement that the three major credit reporting agencies provide consumers with a free copy of their own credit report every 12 months, giving consumers the means to discover and correct errors in them and to check on accounts that may have been fraudulently opened in their names.

2. The creation of a National Fraud Alert System that flags the credit files of consumers or active duty military personnel who reasonably suspect that they have been victimized by identity theft.

2.2 Identity Theft Studies

Using data from 287 users of an online self-assessment tool, who ranged in age from younger than 25 to older than 75, O'Neill and Xiao (2004) performed an empirical study on the frequency of performance of identity theft risk-reduction practices. A key finding of their study was that a majority of respondents did not follow the widely

recommended practices of obtaining a credit report annually to check for errors and

evidence of identity theft, even in states where reports were free of charge (O'Neill & Xiao,

2004).

In their research, demographic variables (income, education, race, and marital

status) were examined to explore differences in frequency of utilizing identity theft risk

reduction practices. A score was assigned based on the identity theft preventive techniques

practiced by the participants. The findings are stated below:

1. Income differences: Lower income consumers had lower scores than

   consumers with higher household incomes (65.4 vs. 74.1), indicating lower

   utilization of identity theft preventive techniques.

2. Educational differences: Participants with lower educational levels were more

   likely to have lower scores when compared to participants with college

   degrees (68.1 vs. 74.8).

3. Racial differences: Non-white respondents had a higher average score than

   whites (74.9 vs. 69.9), indicating more frequent utilization of identity theft

   techniques.

4. Marital status differences: Married consumers were likely to have higher scores

   than singles (73.3 vs. 66.4).

Thus, the authors found that behaviors varied with specific demographic attributes.

Furthermore, they concluded that additional training on identity theft increased awareness

of preventive strategies and led to changes in behavior that could reduce the incidence of

identity theft crime.

Another study on identify theft was conducted by Milne (2003) to measure the self-reported behavior of 61 college students and 59 non-students on thirteen identity theft prevention activities that were suggested by the Federal Trade Commission. Milne found that most of the participants performed the preventive techniques, but noted that additional training and reinforcement were needed. However, Milne did not find statistical differences between student and non-student samples or with respect to demographic attributes such as gender, education, credit card ownership, or shopping behavior (Milne, 2003).

2.3 Effect on Victims

Identity theft victims experience long-term and well-documented pain and suffering, such as harassment from debt collectors, banking problems, loan rejection, utility cut-offs, and arrest (CALPIRG, 2000; ITRC, 2003). Identity theft disrupts the lives of victims and wreaks devastating psychological damage (CALPIRG, 2000). On average, victims spend 600 hours trying to refute negative credit reports and/or false criminal records. In addition, victims are often plagued by increased insurance rates or credit card fees, inability to find a job, higher interest rates, and collection agencies and credit issuers who refuse to clear their records, despite substantiating evidence of the identity theft. The effects on the victim may continue for more than 10 years (ITRC, 2003).

Moreover, research conducted by Titus (1999) found that consumers are often repeat victims, falling prey to identity theft fraud on multiple occasions. This research also demonstrated that individuals, once victimized, are much more likely to be approached again for the same or different types of scams.

A congressional hearing in 1999 on identity theft revealed that police generally did not regard those whose identities had been stolen as true victims, since credit-card companies absorbed the financial loss. The International Association of Chiefs of Police attempted to mitigate this situation as demonstrated by the following:

> "Whereas, reports of identity theft to local law enforcement agencies are often handled with the response 'please contact your credit card company,' and often no official report is created or maintained, causing great difficulty in accounting for and tracing these crimes, and leaving the public with the impression their local police department does not care, ... the International Association of Chiefs of Police call upon all law enforcement agencies in the United States to take more positive actions in recording all incidents of identity theft and referring the victims to the Federal Trade Commission" (International Association of Chiefs of Police, 2000, n.p.).

2.3.1 Effect on Senior Citizens

In 2004, the AARP Public Policy Institute published a report examining the 2003 FTC complaint data from consumers who were over the age of 50, for the use of AARP. This report included data on all senior citizen identity theft crimes reported to the FTC in 2003 and showed a total of 214,905 instances (FTC, 2004a). The report indicated that seniors over the age of 60 were more likely to report several different identity theft crimes than any other "complainant group" (Walters, 2004). Credit card fraud was the most frequently reported identity theft crime, representing 32% of the total. Table 1 shows the breakdown for various types of identity theft crimes reported against seniors in the 2003 report.

Table 1.

FTC Identity Theft Report of Senior Exploitation

Theft Types	Number of Complaints	Percent of All Complaints	Age 50 to 64 Complaints	Age 65+ Complaints
Credit Card Fraud	69,948	32%	12,796 = 40%	5,456 = 44%
Phone or Utilities Fraud	45,548	21%	N/A	N/A
Other Identity Theft Fraud	41,453	19%	N/A	N/A
Bank Fraud	37,412	17%	N/A	N/A
Employment Fraud	23,878	11%	N/A	N/A
Loan Fraud	11,915	6%	N/A	N/A
Government Doc Benefit Fraud	17,483	8%	N/A	N/A
Attempted Identity Theft Fraud	17,110	8%	3839 = 12%	1736 = 14%
Number of Complainants	N= 214,905			

Source: AARP Website (PPI, 2004)

Studies of fraud victims have been few in number and statistical estimates of these crimes are not well represented in the literature (Moore & Mills, 1990). Malks, Schmidt and Austin (2002) found that seniors often do not report financial crimes such as identity theft due to embarrassment, fear and/or dependence upon a financial abuser.

The Titus, Heinzelman and Boyle (1995) survey of seniors suggested that victims often subject themselves to crimes by responding to telemarketing calls. This survey determined that seniors were more likely than young people to be solicited by telemarketers, potentially leading to victimization. Forty-two percent of the seniors reported that they had received 20 or more calls during the past six months for the purpose of soliciting charity contributions, attempting to sell products, or providing notification of a contest or sweepstakes. Fifty-six percent of the victims were over the age of 50.

"These seniors that responded [to the telemarketers] were well-educated, as well as being informed, relatively affluent and not socially isolated. Still, these seniors reported sending in money for participation in a sweepstakes offer or using their credit card" (Titus et al., 1995, p. 70).

Another AARP survey, conducted in 1997, focused on telemarketing and consumers over the age of 50 (AARP, 1996, 1997). Of the 882 seniors surveyed, 52% reported receiving telemarketing calls at least once a week from unknown organizations, asking them to make a donation or an investment, or requesting them to make a purchase. Twelve percent of the sample reported giving their credit card numbers or sending money. This survey was a follow-up to a 1996 AARP survey in which 14% of consumers had reported giving their credit card numbers to unknown organizations.

2.4 Training Methods to Change Attitude and Behaviors

O'Neill and Xiao (2004) and Milne (2003) both identified an educational gap with respect to identity theft prevention and recommended training as a means to prevent these crimes. Titus (1999) suggested that knowledge of identity theft crimes could be helpful in preventing these crimes. Based on his study of victims, Titus concluded that education might have prevented most victims from being susceptible targets. Furthermore, he recommended that training focus on past identity theft victims.

> "Given that a powerful predictor of future victimization is past victimization, more
> targeted campaigns aimed at fraud victims should also be mounted...if the victim's
> action helped the offender commit the crime, then changes in the victim's behavior
> should assist in preventing the crime" (Titus, 1999, p11).

13

Research has demonstrated the impact of training on changing behaviors and attitudes. McConnell, Dwyer and Leening (1996), used direct intervention, teaching low-income residents about the most common causes of fires, in an effort to reduce the incidence of fires at a Memphis Housing Authority complex. Because the training and materials used were tailored to the specific population and their specific living arrangements, the intervention proved successful in changing the behaviors of the residents. A study by Stein (1999) examined the use of a standardized workshop to change the attitudes of students about substance abuse, using a treatment and comparison group to evaluate the impact of the standardized training. Stein's results indicated significant variance in attitudes among different demographic groups, but overall, no significant change occurred as a result of the training. However, in a study conducted by Winge (2003), a training program was developed to teach fifth graders about the hazards of smoking; the training had significant impact on changing their attitudes towards smoking. Additionally, Winge found that when the training was repeated annually, it continued to reinforce the attitudes that prevented children from smoking. All of these findings suggest that to effect meaningful change training must be tailored to the targeted audience. Furthermore, in his research, Glatthorn (1994) analyzed the nature of learning. He determined that meaningful learning is not a passive or receptive process; rather it involves the active use and application of knowledge in solving meaningful problems.

- Meaningful learning involves activating one's prior knowledge and modifying initial understanding of a concept to gain a deeper understanding of the concept.
- Meaningful learning is subjective and personal, with the best learning taking place when the learner internalizes what is being learned.

- Meaningful learning involves carrying out tasks or solving problems that resemble the real world. The best learning tasks are relevant to the learner's needs and authentic with respect to the real world.

- Meaningful learning is social and develops from interacting with others, sharing perceptions, exchanging information, and collaborating in problem solving.

- Meaningful learning is "metacognitive", meaning that one must reflect about one's learning throughout the entire learning process.

- Meaningful learning makes connections; when learners have opportunities to make connections across an integrated curriculum, accelerated teaching and learning can be accomplished.

2.5 Identity Theft Training Program for Seniors

A number of training-based initiatives have been underway in the U.S. to teach senior citizens strategies to help prevent the growing problem of identity theft. For example, Geriatric Education Centers (GEC) formed a national resource network providing education and training to seniors on fraud prevention and elder abuse. Their training sites throughout the country have included nursing homes, adult daycare centers and retirement homes (Parlak & Klein, 1997).

The U.S. Securities and Exchange Commission (SEC) has taken a proactive approach in protecting seniors from identity theft through regulatory and educational efforts. The SEC's initiative has several components, including investor education and assistance, aggressive enforcement of regulations pertaining to investment advisors, and targeted examinations of investment advisors (U.S. Securities and Exchange Commission [SEC], 2006).

Identity theft training programs for seniors are also available online. These include online tutorials provided by AARP and the Better Business Bureau (AARP, 2006; BBB, 2003; FTC, 2005a). The AARP website also contains questions and quizzes to ensure that seniors are learning the material.

CASE: A Faith-Based Program

Faith-based programs reach people not currently served by other efforts. Churches create a sense of community and provide social support (Kloos & Moore, 2000). Senior citizens are more open to discussing their problems when they are in a familiar environment such as their own religious community (Wright, Caserta, & Lund, 2003).

One training program for seniors that works with faith-based organizations is Clergy Against Senior Exploitation (CASE), which originated in Denver, CO. Morrissey and Curtis (2005) cited CASE as a successful and replicable program in part because it relies upon community affiliations to communicate with participants.

Using a "train-the trainer model", local District Attorney's Offices (DAOs) train clergy and the lay leaders of church communities in fraud prevention, who, in turn, train the elderly members of their congregations. This program has been replicated in 26 CASE model sites in the United States. Based on the success of the first model sites, 10 more were added during the summer of 2006, including Anne Arundel County Maryland, which was chosen as a replication site in February 2006. In Maryland, the program was made available for seniors (as opposed to just lay leaders) and adopted the name "Communities Against Senior Exploitation", maintaining the CASE acronym.

The CASE program was designed to bring about awareness of the seriousness of identity theft as a crime against seniors and to educate participants about steps to avoid and report fraud. The training program was developed according to the previously mentioned "Principles of Purposeful Teaching" (Glatthorn, 1994). Thus, it included:

1. facilitated learning,

2. use of a wide range of learning activities,

3. dialogue,

4. real-life stories,

5. a variety of teaching tools,

6. experiential and hands-on learning.

Furthermore, McKenna and Miller (2003) described the CASE program as consisting of three major components:

1. Awareness, including the serious and devastating effects of elder fraud;

2. Content, including the various types of fraud, vulnerabilities of older adults, and prevention steps; and

3. Reinforcement, including follow-up support for clergy and lay leaders by providing notebooks with print materials, emails and Web-based information, and personal support from a Community Advocate.

Moreover, in order to reach churches, synagogues, retirement communities, and other senior-centric communities, local DA offices participating in the CASE program partnered with faith-based fraternal organizations (e.g., Elks, Knights of Columbus) to provide the following:

1. Monthly Fraud Alerts to distribute to the participating organizations;

2. Power Against Fraud seminars for the members;

3. Handbooks and other materials to help older adults and their families avoid fraud and exploitation; and

4. A Fraud Line to assist older adults with crime prevention steps and victim assistance including crisis intervention, emotional support, information and referral, and victim advocacy services

2.6 Opportunity for Contribution to Knowledge

The 2003 study by McKenna and Miller examined the effectiveness of the CASE model, utilizing a post-training survey to evaluate the participants' perceived differences in attitudes and behaviors. Their study provided the basis for continued investigation of the impact of the CASE model.

Although exploratory in nature, this dissertation research extended McKenna and Miller's work by utilizing a quasi-experimental design with comparison groups to measure the changes in attitudes and behaviors which occurred as a result of the CASE training. Specifically, this study focused on the degree of change in attitudes and behaviors that occurred as a result of the training by utilizing a pre- and post-test research design.

This study also attempted to replicate the results of research conducted by O'Neil and Xiao (2004) which demonstrated the impact of training on risk-reduction behaviors by:

1. examining both attitudes and behaviors with respect to identity-theft prevention;

2. using a pre- and post-intervention design and

3. evaluating the differences between a treatment and a comparison group.

Chapter 3

Theoretical Framework

3.1 Theoretical Approach

As discussed in Chapter 2, training is an intervention that has been shown to elicit change in awareness, attitudes and behaviors. However, it has also been shown that in order to optimize the effects of training, the training must be oriented to the specific group of participants. CASE is an example of training program focusing on a specific topic (identity theft) that has been tailored to a specific population (senior citizens) by utilizing partnerships with organizations that the senior citizens trust.

O'Neill and Xiao (2004) provided an approach to identifying and measuring the behaviors that are recommended for preventing identity theft. McKenna and Miller (2003) provided a framework within which the effects of the CASE training on identity theft preventive behaviors could be measured and evaluated. The findings and conclusions of these two studies were the basis for this research.

3.2 Operational Definition of Dependent Variable

The dependent variables in this study were the attitudes, behaviors, and requests for credit card reports after training.

The attitudes studied were those related to:

1. destroying physical evidence that contains personal information (such as bank statements, receipts, credit card offers, etc.);

2. revealing personal information over the phone;

3. protecting outgoing mail; and

4. carrying social security cards.

The behaviors studied were those related to:

1. destroying physical evidence that contains personal information (such as bank statements, receipts, credit card offers, etc.);

2. revealing personal information over the phone;

3. protecting outgoing mail;

4. carrying social security cards; and

5. ordering credit reports.

3.3 Operational Definition of the Independent Variable

The independent variable in this study was the CASE training, as delivered to a treatment group of senior citizens.

3.4 Research Questions Guiding Study

This exploratory research was guided by the following research questions:

1. Is there a relationship between participation in the CASE training program and attitudes towards identity theft prevention?

2. Is there a relationship between participation in the CASE training program and the use of identity theft prevention behaviors?

3. Is there a relationship between participation in CASE training program and the practice of ordering a credit report?

3.5 Alternative Explanation for Changes

Factors other than training can affect the awareness, attitudes and behaviors of senior citizens towards identity theft. An example of a plausible alternative explanation for such changes is the effect of a major external identity theft event occurrence.

One such event was the Designer Shoe Warehouse (DSW) credit card theft in which 1.4 million credit card and debit card numbers were stolen from the DSW database between November 2004 and February 2005 (DSW, 2005). This event received a great deal of media attention, including information on the benefits of ordering credit reports (ABC7Chicago.com, 2005) and therefore could have influenced the attitudes and behaviors of those who were exposed to it.

Chapter 4

Research Methodology

4.1 Project History

As a result of personal relationships with senior citizens in the church community, the researcher was exposed to the devastating losses experienced by victims of identity theft. This led the researcher to conduct a preliminary research literature review focusing on this crime and its impact on senior citizens, in particular. As mentioned previously, this review revealed that training had been used successfully to affect behavior which could help to prevent identity theft.

A specific example of this was the CASE Training Program, developed by the District Attorney's Office (DAO) in Denver, Colorado, to educate seniors through their church organizations, about the crime of identity theft. Upon learning of this program, the researcher contacted the Denver DAO and was referred to Kristin Riggins, the CASE representative, with the DAO of Anne Arundel County, Maryland. Ms. Riggins was scheduled to conduct an upcoming CASE training seminar at St. Philip's Episcopal (SPE) Church in Annapolis, Maryland. The CASE representative referred the researcher to the Rev. Angela Sheppard to gain permission for her congregation to participate in this dissertation study. Additionally, Ms. Riggins arranged for Heritage Baptist (HB) Church, also in Annapolis, to participate as a second treatment group.

4.2 Context of Study

4.2.1 Setting

In this study, two treatment groups and two comparison groups of senior citizens were utilized. Later, for data analysis purposes, these groups were combined into a single treatment group and a single comparison group.

As mentioned previously, the two treatment groups were volunteer members of St. Philip's Episcopal Church (SPE) and Heritage Baptist (HB) Church who were attending the CASE training program. In addition, the researcher arranged for volunteers from the Mt. Pleasant Baptist (MPB) Church in Aldie, Virginia and the Wingler House (WH) Chapel in Ashburn, Virginia, to participate in the two comparison groups which would not receive training.

The first CASE identity theft training seminar was taught in the activity room of the SPE Church, in Annapolis, MD on May 17, 2006, with the researcher present. The pre-treatment survey (O1) was administered on the day of the training, just prior to the seminar. The researcher returned two weeks later on May 31, 2006 to administer a post-treatment survey (O2) and to conduct follow-up interviews.

The second CASE identity theft training seminar took place in the activity room of the HB Church, also in Annapolis, on June 20, 2006. As with the first treatment group, a pre-treatment survey (O1) was administered by the researcher just prior to the seminar on the day of the training session. Two weeks later, on July 5, 2006, a post-treatment survey (O2) was administered and follow-up interviews were conducted by the researcher.

The participants in the first comparison group (who received no CASE training) were volunteer residents of Wingler House (WH) who attended church there. WH is a retirement community located in Ashburn, Virginia, a suburban area 40 miles outside of the greater Washington Metro area. The pre-treatment survey (O1), identical to the one that had been administered to both treatment groups, was administered to the first comparison group on May 17, 2006. Then on May 31, 2006, a follow-up survey (O2), identical to the post-treatment survey that had been administered to the treatment groups, was administered to this comparison group and interviews were conducted by the researcher.

The second comparison group, who also received no training, was comprised of volunteer church members from the MPB Church in Aldie, Virginia, a suburb located 60 miles outside of the greater Washington Metro area. The pre-treatment survey (O1), identical to the one which had been administered to the treatment groups, was administered to this group on June 18, 2006. Two weeks later, on July 9, 2006, a follow-up survey (O2), identical to the post-treatment survey administered to the treatment groups, was administered to this group and interviews were conducted by the researcher.

4.2.2 Population

All participants in this research, whether in the treatment or comparison groups, were at least 50 years of age. The study sample consisted of 57 participants, including 23 treatment subjects and 34 comparison subjects. The treatment and comparison groups were similar in both age and gender. (Additional demographic information with respect to the study sample is provided in Chapter 5.)

Table 2 shows the observation dates and gender distribution within the treatment and comparison groups.

Table 2.
Observation Dates (O1 & O2) and Gender Distribution

				Sample Size		
Groups	**Church**	**Observation 01**	**Observation 02**	**Men**	**Women**	**Total**
TG1	**St. Philips**	5/17/06	5/31/06	0	9	**23**
TG2	**Heritage**	6/20/06	07/05/06	6	8	
CG1	**Wingler**	05/17/06	05/31/06	0	8	**34**
CG2	**Mt. Pleasant**	06/18/06	07/09/06	10	16	

4.2.3 Limitations

This study had two major limitations. First, it utilized a small, non-representative sample size and second, it utilized convenience samples consisting of voluntary, (self-selected) participants, rather than randomly selected samples. However, these limitations did not jeopardize the validity of the research findings, because the study makes no claims of generalizability.

4.2.4 Delimitations

In addition to the limitations identified above, the researcher placed the following delimitations on the study: a) Subjects who did not identify English as their first language were eliminated from the sample to reduce the risk of misinterpretation. b) Participants came solely from congregations of St. Philip's Episcopal Church, Heritage Baptist Church, Mt Pleasant Baptist Church or the Wingler House Chapel.

4.3 Data Collection

This research utilized a pre-observation and post-observation design with treatment and comparison groups. The first observation (O1) was a survey administered prior to the CASE training. The second observation (O2) was administered two weeks after the first and follow-up interviews were conducted at that time. The treatment group participated in the CASE training; the comparison group did not.

4.4 Intervention

The CASE Training was delivered in an informal setting using lecture-based instruction. The length of the sessions ranged from one to two hours, depending upon the level of interaction which occurred in the group. In addition, participants received an Identity Theft Handbook, prepared by CASE, which contained guidelines, techniques, and contact information, a necklace wallet, and a recent Security Alerts issued by the DAO (see Appendix F).

4.5 Instrumentation

4.5.1 Surveys

The O1 and O2 surveys were based on risk reduction strategies suggested in Federal Trade Commission publications (FTC, 2000, 2003) and an online Identity Theft IQ Test (Privacy Rights Clearinghouse, 2003). The survey instruments are found in Appendix B. The O1 survey contained 13 demographic questions, 10 questions measuring attitudes and 10 questions measuring behaviors. The O2 survey contained ten questions measuring attitudes, ten questions measuring behaviors and six more open-ended questions, which

27

were posed again during the interview, in order to gain insight into the survey responses. These questions are described below.

The O1 survey was designed to determine the awareness, knowledge, and behavior of both treatment and comparison groups with respect to identity theft. The O2 survey was designed to determine their awareness, knowledge and behavior of these groups two weeks later.

4.5.2 Interviews

Six additional interview questions (matching the O2 survey questions) were asked of both treatment and comparison group participants, at the conclusion of the O2 survey, to gain further insight into survey responses.

The questions were as follows:

1. In the past two weeks, have you ordered a credit report? If so, what made you order the report?

2. What form of identity theft do you think is the worst and why?

3. Are you less concerned about identity theft today than you were two weeks ago?

4. Do you carry your social security card with you and why?

5. Does your spouse worry more about identity theft more than you do? Are most of your bills in your spouse's name?

6. To what extent has the recent Veteran's Administration computer theft affected your attitudes and behaviors?

4.6 Methodology

The researcher utilized a quasi-experimental design with both treatment and comparison groups formed through convenience sampling. This design, frequently called the non-equivalent comparison group design, was utilized with a treatment group and an untreated comparison group, with both pre-test and post-test data collected.

The pre-test and the comparison group were both utilized to help mitigate the risks associated with non-laboratory based studies. The most common of these are selection bias, and the possibility of an external event occurring during the treatment period that affects one group more than another.

The protocol was as follows:

1. First survey (O1) administered to both treatment and comparison groups;

2. Training conducted for treatment group only and

3. Second survey (O2) and interviews conducted for both treatment and comparison groups.

Chapter 5

Analysis of Data

5.1 Overview

This chapter contains an analysis of the data collected. In order to more easily analyze the data, the two treatment groups and the two comparison groups were combined into a single treatment group and a single comparison group.

The demographic characteristics of the data sample are presented first, followed by the pre-intervention analysis (O1), the post-intervention analysis (O2), and, finally, a comparison of the pre-intervention and post-intervention data (O1 and O2). The data analysis in each section is divided into the two areas of investigation: attitudes and behaviors.

The data analysis was performed by utilizing only the responses in the "Strongly Agree" column. Due to their importance in identity theft prevention the responses to Items 7 and 10, which relate to carrying a social security card, are analyzed in each section.

Some tables, in this chapter, contain comparative analyses with respect to the level of change that occurred between O1 and O2. In those instances, a rating was assigned according to the level of change that occurred. A percentage change of 0% to 9% was designated "Low"; a percentage change of 10% to 19% was designated "Medium" and a percentage change of 20% or more was designated "High".

5.2 Demographic Characteristics of Sample

5.2.1 Gender

Female participants represented 74% of the total treatment group population (including the SPE treatment group which was 100% female). In the comparison group population, approximately 75% of all participants were also female (including the WH comparison group which was 100% female).

Tables 3 and 4 summarize the gender distribution of the treatment and comparison groups, respectively.

Table 3.
Gender Distribution of Treatment Group

	SPE (St. Philips)		HB (Heritage Baptist)		Total Treatment	
Gender	Count	Percentage	Count	Percentage	Count	Percentage
Male	0	0.0	6	42.9	6	26.1
Female	9	100.0	8	57.1	17	73.9
Total	9	100.0	14	100.0	23	100.0

Table 4.
Gender Distribution of Comparison Group

	WH (Wingler House)		MPB (Mt Pleasant Baptist)		Total Comparison	
Gender	Count	Percentage	Count	Percentage	Count	Percentage
Male	0	0.0	10	38.5	10	29.4
Female	8	100.0	16	61.5	24	70.6
Total	8	100.0	26	100.0	34	100.0

5.2.2 Income

Tables 5 and 6 summarize the income distribution of the treatment and comparison groups, respectively. The largest portion of the treatment group (47.8%) reported incomes between $50K and $99K, followed by those reporting incomes between $25K and $49K

(30.4%). Only a small minority (4.3%) of the treatment group reported incomes of less than $25K or greater than $100K (17.3%).

In contrast, the largest portion of the comparison group (47.1%) reported incomes between $25K and $49K. The remainder of the comparison group was almost evenly distributed between those reporting incomes of less than $25K (23.5%) and those reporting incomes between $50K and $99K (29.4%). In the comparison group, no income over $100K was reported.

Table 5.
Income Distribution of Treatment Group

	SPE (St. Philips)		HB (Heritage Baptist)		Total Treatment	
Income	**Count**	**Percentage**	**Count**	**Percentage**	**Count**	**Percentage**
< $25 K	1	11.1	0	0.0	1	4.3
$25K – $49K	5	55.6	2	14.3	7	30.4
$50K – $99K	3	33.3	8	57.1	11	47.8
$100K >	0	0.0	4	28.6	4	17.3
Total	**9**	**100.0**	**14**	**100.0**	**23**	**100.0**

Table 6.
Income Distribution of Comparison Group

	WH (Wingler House)		MPB (Mt Pleasant Baptist)		Total Comparison	
Income	**Count**	**Percentage**	**Count**	**Percentage**	**Count**	**Percentage**
< $25 K	3	37.5	5	19.2	8	23.5
$25K – $49K	4	50.0	12	46.1	16	47.1
$50K – $99K	1	12.5	9	34.6	10	29.4
$100K >	0	0.0	0	0.0	0	0.0
Total	**8**	**100.0**	**26**	**100.0**	**34**	**100.0**

5.2.3 Marital Status

Tables 7 and 8 summarize the marital status of the treatment and comparison group participants, respectively. The majority of the treatment group participants were married

(65%). Approximately 17% of the treatment group participants were widowed. A small minority (8.7%) of the treatment group participants were divorced; no participants in the treatment group reported being single.

Most of the comparison group participants reported being married (44%). The portion of the comparison group who reported being widowed was 32.3%, while the percentage who reported being widowed in the treatment group was only 17.4%. The comparison group had more divorced participants (14.4%) than did the treatment group (8.7%). In addition, the comparison group had a few single members (8.8%) as compared to the treatment group which had none. There were more divorced members in the comparison group (14.7%) as compared to the treatment group (8.7%).

Table 7.
Marital Status Distribution of Treatment Group

Marital Status	SPE (St. Philips)		HB (Heritage Baptist)		Total Treatment	
	Count	Percentage	Count	Percentage	Count	Percentage
Single	0	0.0	0	0.0	0	0.0
Married	3	33.3	12	85.7	15	65.2
Divorced	2	22.2	0	0.0	2	8.7
Widowed	4	44.4	2	14.3	6	26.1
Total	9	100.0	14	100.0	23	100.0

Table 8.
Marital Status Distribution of Comparison Group

Marital Status	WH (Wingler House)		MPB (Mt Pleasant Baptist)		Total Comparison	
	Count	Percentage	Count	Percentage	Count	Percentage
Single	0	0.0	3	11.5	3	8.8
Married	0	0.0	15	57.7	15	44.1
Divorced	1	12.5	4	15.4	5	14.7
Widowed	7	87.5	4	15.4	11	32.3
Total	8	100.0	26	100.0	34	100.0

5.2.4 Education

Tables 9 and 10 summarize the educational levels of the treatment and comparison group participants, respectively. The treatment group participants were approximately equal in their distribution across three categories of education: High School/GED (34.8%), BS (26.1%) and Masters (30.4%).

The comparison group exhibited a significantly different distribution across the three categories, with almost 60% reporting a high school or GED as their highest education level. Twenty percent of the comparison group reported their education as something other than the three categories identified.

Table 9.
Education Distribution of Treatment Group

Education	SPE (St. Philips)		HB (Heritage Baptist)		Total Treatment	
	Count	Percentage	Count	Percentage	Count	Percentage
High/GED	3	33.3	5	35.7	8	34.8
Bachelor	3	33.3	3	21.4	6	26.1
MS	3	33.3	4	28.6	7	30.4
Ph D	0	0.0	1	7.1	1	4.3
Other	0	0.0	1	7.1	1	4.3
Total	9	100.0	14	100.0	23	100.0

Table 10.
Education Distribution of Comparison Group

Education	WH (Wingler House)		MPB (Mt Pleasant Baptist)		Total Comparison	
	Count	Percentage	Count	Percentage	Count	Percentage
High/GED	4	50.0	16	61.5	20	58.8
Bachelor	2	25.0	3	11.5	5	14.7
MS	2	25.0	0	0.0	2	5.9
Ph D	0	0.0	0	0.0	0	0.0
Other	0	0.0	7	26.9	7	20.6
Total	8	100.0	26	100.0	34	100.0

5.2.5 Race

Tables 11 and 12 summarize the racial composition of the treatment and comparison group participants, respectively. In the treatment group, the majority of the participants were Caucasian (65%), one third of the participants were Black (30%) and a small minority (4.3%) was Hispanic. In contrast, the vast majority of the comparison group participants were Black (77%). Less than one fifth of the comparison group participants were Caucasian (18%). Less than five percent of the comparison group participants reported being Hispanic or Native American.

Table 11.
Race Distribution of Treatment Group

	SPE (St. Philips)		HB (Heritage Baptist)		Total Treatment	
Race	Count	Percentage	Count	Percentage	Count	Percentage
Caucasian	1	11.1	14	100.0	15	65.2
Hispanic	1	11.1	0	0.0	1	4.3
Black	7	77.7	0	0.0	7	30.4
Native American	0	0.0	0	0.0	0	0.0
Total	9	100.0	14	100.0	23	100.0

Table 12.
Race Distribution of Comparison Group

	WH (Wingler House)		MPB (Mt Pleasant Baptist)		Total Comparison	
Race	Count	Percentage	Count	Percentage	Count	Percentage
Caucasian	6	75.0	0	0.0	6	17.6
Hispanic	0	0.0	1	3.8	1	2.9
Black	2	25.0	24	92.3	26	76.5
Native American	0	0.0	1	3.8	1	2.9
Total	8	100.0	26	100.0	34	100.0

5.2.6 Internet Access

Tables 13 and 14 summarize the level of Internet access of the treatment and comparison group participants, respectively. Over 80% of the treatment group participants reported having Internet access (83%). In contrast, less than half of the comparison group participants reported having Internet access (44%).

Table 13.
Internet Access Distribution of Treatment Group

	SPE (St. Philips)		HB (Heritage Baptist)		Total Treatment	
Internet Access	Count	Percentage	Count	Percentage	Count	Percentage
Yes	6	66.7	13	92.9	19	82.6
No	3	33.3	1	7.1	4	17.4
Total	**9**	**100.0**	**14**	**100.0**	**23**	**100.0**

Table 14.
Internet Access Distribution of Comparison Group

	WH (Wingler House)		MPB (Mt Pleasant Baptist)		Total Comparison	
Internet Access	Count	Percentage	Count	Percentage	Count	Percentage
Yes	0	0.0	15	57.7	15	44.1
No	8	100.0	11	42.3	19	55.9
Total	**8**	**100.0**	**26**	**100.0**	**34**	**100.0**

5.3 Observation 1 Analysis

5.3.1 Treatment Group

The pre-intervention treatment survey (O1) measured the attitudes and behaviors of the treatment group participants, prior to participation in the CASE training. Table 15 shows the frequency distribution of item responses to this survey by the treatment group participants.

The data suggest that approximately half of the treatment group participants (51.35%) used identity theft prevention techniques prior to the training, although a larger percentage (67.78%) indicated positive attitudes towards these behaviors. There was a wide range of responses for the "Strongly Agree" category for items related to attitudes (35% to 87%). Responses related to behavior items spanned an even wider range (26% to 87%).

Items 7A and 7B of the survey stated, "I should not reveal my social security number to telemarketers". The majority of participants (83%) indicated strong agreement with this statement in the attitude part of the survey. The results were similar in the responses to the behaviors section (87%). With only a four percent difference in the responses, the reported attitudes and behaviors with respect to revealing the social security number to telemarketers quite consistent.

Items 10A and 10B of the survey addressed protection of social security numbers, ("I do not carry my social security card in my wallet or purse"). Seventy percent of the participants strongly agreed with this statement; however, only 40% of responses by the participants indicated that they practiced this behavior. Thus, there was a 30% gap between attitudes and behaviors reported.

37

Table 15.

Treatment Group: Observation 1 Survey Analysis (TO1)

	N=23	Strongly Agree	Moderately Agree	Moderately Disagree	Strongly Disagree
	Attitude				
1A	Should destroy bank statements	73.91%	17.39%	4.34%	4.34%
2A	Should destroy credit card receipts	78.26%	17.39%	4.34%	4.34%
3A	Should destroy pre-approved credit card offers	86.95%	13.04%	0.00%	0.00%
4A	Should destroy old personal correspondence.	34.78%	39.13%	17.39%	8.69%
5A	Should destroy pay stubs	65.21%	4.34%	4.34%	0.00%
6A	Should destroy old utility bills	47.83%	30.43%	21.74%	0.00%
7A	Should not reveal social security number	82.61%	13.04%	0.00%	4.34%
8A	Should place out-going mail in mailbox	60.87%	30.34%	0.00%	8.69%
9A	Should not give out contact information	78.26%	21.74%	0.00%	0.00%
10A	Should carry my social security card	69.56%	26.08%	0.00%	4.34%
	Average Attitude	**67.78%**	**21.24%**	**5.22%**	**3.47%**
	Behavior				
1B	Destroy bank statements	47.83%	21.74%	21.74%	8.69%
2B	Destroy credit card receipts	60.87%	17.90%	17.39%	0.00%
3B	Destroy pre-approved credit card offers	82.61%	4.34%	8.69%	4.34%
4B	Destroy old personal correspondence	26.08%	26.08%	21.74%	26.08%
5B	Destroy pay stubs	43.47%	30.43%	13.04%	13.04%
6B	Destroy old utility bills	43.47%	13.04%	17.39%	26.08%
7B	Do not reveal social security number	86.95%	8.69%	4.34%	0.00%
8B	Place out-going mail in secure mailbox	30.43%	39.10%	21.74%	8.69%
9B	Do not give out contact information	52.17%	8.69%	8.69%	30.43%
10B	Do not carry my social security card	39.60%	8.69%	13.04%	39.10%
	Average Behavior	**51.35%**	**19.17%**	**14.78**	**15.65%**

Other disparities between attitudes and behaviors were exhibited with respect to the following items: destroying bank statements, destroying old pay stubs, placing out-going mail in a secure mailbox, and not giving out personal contact information. Detailed differences between attitudes and behaviors are described as follows:

- Secure out-going mail: While 61% of the participants strongly agreed with placing out-going mail in a secure mailbox, only 30% reported doing so. The percentage gap between attitude and behavior was 31%.

- Personal contact information: While 78% of the participants strongly agreed that personal contact information should not be given out, only 52% reported behavior consistent with this. The percentage gap between attitude and behavior was 26%.

- Bank statements: While 74% of the participants strongly agreed that bank statements should be destroyed, only 48% reported doing so. The percentage gap between attitude and behavior was 26%.

- Old pay stubs: While 65% of the participants strongly agreed that old pay stubs should be destroyed, only 43% reported doing so. The percentage gap between attitude and behavior was 22%.

5.3.2 Comparison Group

The pre-intervention survey (O1) was administered to the comparison group participants who received no training. Table 16 contains the frequency distribution of item responses to this survey by the comparison group participants.

The data suggested that slightly more than half of the participants (58.82%) used the identity theft prevention techniques prior to the survey. The responses by the comparison group in the "Strongly Agree" category for attitude items ranged from 55% to 94%. The responses for this group in the "Strongly Agree" category for behavior items ranged from 32% to 82%.

For Items 7A and 7B, which related to not revealing social security numbers to telemarketers, 79% strongly agreed with the statement in the attitude part of the survey, while 82% of the group indicated agreement in the behavior section; thus attitudes and behaviors for these items were fairly consistent. However, with respect to Items 10A and 10B of the survey, which related to not carrying a social security card, 56% strongly agreed with the statement, but only 32% of participants strongly agreed with the behavior. Thus, there was a gap of 24% between attitudes and behaviors.

In addition, there were differences between attitudes and behaviors reported by comparison group participants, for the following items: destroying pre-approved credit card offers, destroying old personal correspondence, destroying old pay stubs, and destroying old utility bills. Detailed differences are described as follows:

- Old personal correspondence: While 79% of the participants strongly agreed that old personal correspondence should be destroyed, only 47% reported doing so. The percentage gap between attitude and behavior was 32%.

- Old pay stubs: While 71% of the participants strongly agreed that old pay stubs should be destroyed, only 43% reported doing so. The percentage gap between attitude and behavior was 27%.

- Old utility bills: While 68% of the participants strongly agreed that old utility bills should be destroyed, only 45% reported doing so. The percentage gap between attitude and behavior was 23%.

- Pre-approved credit card offers: While 94% of the participants strongly agreed that pre-approved credit card offers should be destroyed, only 74% reported doing so. The percentage gap between attitude and behavior was 20%.

Table 16.

Comparison Group: Observation 1 Survey Analysis (CO1)

	N=34	Strongly Agree	Moderately Agree	Moderately Disagree	Strongly Disagree
	Attitude				
1A	Should destroy bank statements	74.28%	5.88%	8.82%	8.82%
2A	Should destroy credit card receipts	79.41%	8.82%	8.82%	2.94%
3A	Should destroy pre-approved credit card offers	94.10%	5.88%	0.00%	0.00%
4A	Should destroy old personal correspondence.	79.41%	8.82%	5.88%	5.88%
5A	Should destroy pay stubs	70.58%	14.70%	5.88%	8.82%
6A	Should destroy old utility bills	67.64%	11.76%	8.82%	11.76%
7A	Should not reveal social security number	79.41%	5.88%	0.00%	14.71%
8A	Should place out-going mail in mailbox	70.58%	14.70%	5.88%	8.82%
9A	Should not give out contact information	79.41%	2.94%	2.94%	14.71%
10A	Should carry my social security card	55.88%	5.88%	11.76%	26.47%
	Average Attitude	**75.06%**	**8.53%**	**5.88%**	**10.29%**
	Behavior				
1B	Destroy bank statements	61.76%	14.70%	14.71%	8.82%
2B	Destroy credit card receipts	61.76%	11.76%	14.71%	11.76%
3B	Destroy pre-approved credit card offers	74.28%	8.82%	5.88%	8.82%
4B	Destroy old personal correspondence	47.06%	26.47%	17.74%	8.82%
5B	Destroy pay stubs	42.86%	29.41%	8.82%	20.59%
6B	Destroy old utility bills	44.71%	20.59%	5.88%	14.71%
7B	Do not reveal social security number	82.23%	0.00%	0.00%	11.76%
8B	Place out-going mail in secure mailbox	67.64%	8.82%	5.88%	6.00%
9B	Do not give out contact information	73.52%	2.94%	11.76%	11.76%
10B	Do not carry my social security card	32.35%	8.82%	8.82%	50.00%
	Average Behavior	**58.81%**	**13.23%**	**9.42%**	**15.30%**

5.3.3 Analysis of Differences Between Groups in O1 Responses

This section compares the O1 responses of the treatment group with the O1 responses of the comparison group.

Attitudes

The O1 responses, as shown in Table 17, indicated that the attitudes and behaviors of the treatment group and the comparison group participants were similar with respect to identity theft. As seen in Table 18, this was true for eight of the ten survey items. However, for two items the groups exhibited disparity in their responses; these were "destroying old utility bills" and "destroying old personal correspondence". With respect to the latter, 44% more of the comparison group responded with a "Strongly Agree" response than did the treatment group. With respect to the former, 21% more of the comparison group responded with "Strongly Agree" than did the treatment group.

Behaviors

The O1 responses also demonstrated similarity between the behaviors of the treatment and comparison group participants. As seen in Table 17, this was true with respect to seven of the ten survey items. However, there were three items for which the two groups did exhibit differences in their responses; these were "destroying old personal correspondence "(21%), "placing out-going mail in a secure mailbox" (38%) and "giving out contact information" (22%).

Table 17.
Between Group Analysis: TO1 & CO1

		Treatment	Comparison	Difference	
	Attitude	**TO1**	**CO1**		
1A	Should destroy bank statements	74%	74%	0%	None
2A	Should destroy credit card receipts	78%	79%	+ 1%	Low
3A	Should destroy pre-approved credit card offers	87%	94%	+ 7%	Low
4A	Should destroy old personal correspondence.	35%	79%	+ 44%	High
5A	Should destroy pay stubs	65%	71%	+ 5%	Low
6A	Should destroy old utility bills	48%	68%	+ 21%	High
7A	Should not reveal social security number	83%	79%	- 4%	Low
8A	Should place out-going mail in mailbox	61%	71%	+ 10%	Low
9A	Should not give out contact information	78%	79%	+ 1%	Low
10A	Should carry my social security card	70%	56%	-16%	Med
	Comparative Total Average	**68%**	**75%**	**+ 7**	**Low**
	Behavior				
1B	Destroy bank statements	48%	62%	+ 14%	Med
2B	Destroy credit card receipts	61%	62%	+ 1%	Low
3B	Destroy pre-approved credit card offers	83%	74%	- 9%	Low
4B	Destroy old personal correspondence	26%	47%	+ 21%	High
5B	Destroy pay stubs	43%	43%	0%	None
6B	Destroy old utility bills	43%	45%	+ 2%	Low
7B	Do not reveal social security number	87%	82%	- 5%	Low
8B	Place out-going mail in secure mailbox	30%	68%	+ 38%	High
9B	Do not give out contact information	52%	74%	+ 22%	High
10B	Do not carry my social security card	40%	32%	- 8%	Low
	Comparative Total Average	**51%**	**59%**	**+ 8%**	**Low**

5.4 Observation 2 Analysis

5.4.1 Treatment Group

The second observation (O2) survey was administered to the treatment group two weeks after the intervention (CASE training). Table 18 contains the frequency distribution of item responses to the post-intervention survey (O2) by the treatment group participants. An average of 69.79% of the respondents indicated the use of identity theft prevention behaviors after the training. In the treatment group, the O2 responses in the "Strongly Agree" category, for items related to attitudes, ranged from 61% to 96% of the participants, while the responses related to behavior in the "Strongly Agree" category ranged from 48% to 92%.

For Items 7A and 7B (not revealing social security numbers to telemarketers), 82.6% strongly agreed in the attitudes section and 91.3% strongly agreed in the behavior section, indicating consistency between the attitudes and behaviors of the participants. For Items 10A and 10B, 78.26% strongly agreed with not carrying a social security card in the attitude survey, while 82.6% strongly agreed with this item in the behavior section, again indicating consistency between attitudes and behaviors.

However, there was a significant gap between attitudes and behaviors with respect to two items: destroying bank statements and destroying credit card receipts. These differences are described as follows:

- Credit card receipts: While 96% of the participants strongly agreed that bank credit card receipts should be destroyed, only 70% reported doing so. The percentage gap between attitude and behavior was 26%.

- Bank statements: While 83% of the participants strongly agreed that bank statements should be destroyed, only 59% reported doing so behavior. The percentage gap between attitude and behavior was 24%.

5.4.2 Comparison Group

A follow-up survey (O2) was administered to the comparison group two weeks after the O1 survey had been administered. Table 19 contains the frequency distribution of item responses by the comparison group participants. An average of 65.42% of the respondents indicated the use of identity theft prevention behaviors, without the benefit of the training intervention.

In the comparison group, the O2 responses in the "Strongly Agree" category for items related to attitudes ranged from 53% to 91% of the participants, while the responses related to behavior in the "Strongly Agree" category ranged from 44% to 82%.

For Items 7A and 7B, (not revealing social security numbers to telemarketers), 79.41% strongly agreed in the attitude section and 82.23% strongly agreed in the behavior section, indicating consistency between the attitudes and behaviors of the participants. For Items 10A and 10B, 52.94% of the participants strongly agreed with not carrying a social security card in the attitude section, while 44.11% strongly agreed with this item in the behavior section, again indicating consistency between attitudes and behaviors.

Based upon their survey responses, there were no significant differences reported in the attitudes and behaviors of the comparison group participants.

Table 18.

Treatment Group: Observation 2 Survey Analysis (TO2)

	N=23	Strongly Agree	Moderately Agree	Moderately Disagree	Strongly Disagree
	Attitude				
1A	Should destroy bank statements	82.60%	13.04%	4.34%	0.00%
2A	Should destroy credit card receipts	95.65%	4.34%	0.00%	0.00%
3A	Should destroy pre-approved credit card offers	95.65%	4.34%	0.00%	0.00%
4A	Should destroy old personal correspondence.	60.86%	26.08%	13.04%	0.00%
5A	Should destroy pay stubs	69.56%	26.08%	4.34%	0.00%
6A	Should destroy old utility bills	60.86%	26.08%	8.69%	4.34%
7A	Should not reveal social security number	82.60%	8.69%	0.00%	8.69%
8A	Should place out-going mail in mailbox	73.91%	13.04%	4.34%	13.04%
9A	Should not give out contact information	86.95%	13.04%	0.00%	0.00%
10A	Should carry my social security card	78.26%	13.04%	0.00%	8.69%
	Average Attitude	**78.69%**	**14.78%**	**3.48%**	**3.48%**
	Behavior				
1B	Destroy bank statements	58.82%	8.69%	26.08%	13.04%
2B	Destroy credit card receipts	69.56%	8.69%	17.39	4.34%
3B	Destroy pre-approved credit card offers	86.96%	8.69%	4.34%	0.00%
4B	Destroy old personal correspondence	47.83%	26.08%	4.34%	21.74%
5B	Destroy pay stubs	56.52%	17.39%	13.04%	13.04%
6B	Destroy old utility bills	52.17%	13.04%	13.04%	21.74%
7B	Do not reveal social security number	91.30%	4.34%	0.00%	4.34%
8B	Place out-going mail in secure mailbox	56.52%	13.04%	17.39%	13.04%
9B	Do not give out contact information	95.65%	0.00%	4.34%	0.00%
10B	Do not carry my social security card	82.60%	8.69%	0.00%	8.69%
	Average Behavior	**69.79%**	**10.87%**	**10.00%**	**10.00%**

Table 19.

Comparison Group: Observation 2 Surveys Analysis (CO2)

	N=34	Strongly Agree	Moderately Agree	Moderately Disagree	Strongly Disagree
	Attitude				
1A	Should destroy bank statements	70.58%	11.76%	2.94%	14.71%
2A	Should destroy credit card receipts	91.18%	0.00%	2.94%	5.88%
3A	Should destroy pre-approved credit card offers	82.23%	2.94%	2.94%	5.88%
4A	Should destroy old personal correspondence.	67.64%	11.76%	11.76%	8.82%
5A	Should destroy pay stubs	69.56%	20.59%	5.88%	14.70%
6A	Should destroy old utility bills	55.89%	26.47%	8.82%	8.82%
7A	Should not reveal social security number	79.41%	8.82%	0.00%	11.76%
8A	Should place out-going mail in mailbox	82.23%	2.94%	5.88%	2.94%
9A	Should not give out contact information	73.52%	17.64%	2.94%	5.88%
10A	Should not carry my social security card	52.94%	20.59%	14.70%	11.76%
	Average Attitude	**72.52%**	**12.35%**	**5.88%**	**9.12%**
	Behavior				
1B	Destroy bank statements	58.82%	23.52%	2.94%	14.70%
2B	Destroy credit card receipts	74.28%	8.82%	2.94%	11.76%
3B	Destroy pre-approved credit card offers	74.28%	8.82%	0.00%	14.70%
4B	Destroy old personal correspondence	52.94%	20.59%	14.70%	11.76%
5B	Destroy pay stubs	55.89%	26.47%	8.82%	8.82%
6B	Destroy old utility bills	50%	26.49%	8.82%	14.70%
7B	Do not reveal social security number	82.23%	2.94%	0.00%	8.82%
8B	Place out-going mail in secure mailbox	79.41%	11.76%	2.94%	5.88%
9B	Do not give out contact information	82.23%	11.76%	0.00%	0.00%
10B	Do not carry my social security card	44.11%	11.76%	14.70%	29.41%
	Average Behavior	**65.42%**	**15.29%**	**5.59%**	**12.06%**

5.4.3 Analysis of Differences Between Groups in O2 Responses

This section compares the O2 survey responses by the treatment group with the O2 responses by the comparison group. As shown in Table 20, in their O2 responses, the treatment group reported higher levels of positive attitudes and behaviors with respect to identity theft prevention than did the comparison group.

Attitudes

The percentage of O2 responses by the treatment group in the "Strongly Agree" category with respect to attitudes was 6.3% higher than it was *in the comparison group.* For Item 7A which states "should not reveal social security number", the percentage of O2 responses in the "Strongly Agree" category was 4% higher than it was in the comparison group.

However, with respect to Item 10A, which states, "should not carry my social security card", there was a more significant difference between the two groups. For this item, in the treatment group, the percentage of O2 responses in the "Strongly Agree" category was 25% higher than it was in the comparison group.

Table 20.
Between Group Analysis: TO2 & CO2

		Treatment	Comparison	Difference	
	Attitude	**TO2**	**CO2**		
1A	Should destroy bank statements	83%	71%	+ 12%	Med
2A	Should destroy credit card receipts	96%	91%	+ 5%	Low
3A	Should destroy pre-approved credit card offers	96%	82%	+ 14%	Med
4A	Should destroy old personal correspondence	61%	68%	- 7%	Low
5A	Should destroy pay stubs	70%	70%	0%	Low
6A	Should destroy old utility bills	61%	56%	+ 5%	Low
7A	Should not reveal social security number	83%	79%	+ 4%	Low
8A	Should place out-going mail in mailbox	74%	82%	- 8%	Low
9A	Should not give out contact information	87%	74%	+ 13%	Med
10A	Should not carry my social security card	78%	53%	+ 25%	High
	Average Attitude	**79%**	**73%**	**6 %**	**Low**
	Behavior				
1B	Destroy bank statements	59%	59%	0%	
2B	Destroy credit card receipts	70%	74%	- 4%	Low
3B	Destroy pre-approved credit card offers	87%	74%	+ 13%	Med
4B	Destroy old personal correspondence	48%	53%	- 5%	Low
5B	Destroy pay stubs	57%	56%	+ 1%	Low
6B	Destroy old utility bills	52%	50%	+ 2%	Low
7B	Do not reveal social security number	91%	82%	+ 9%	Med
8B	Place out-going mail in secure mailbox	57%	79%	- 22%	High
9B	Do not give out contact information	96%	82%	+ 14%	Med
10B	Do not carry my social security card	83%	44%	+ 39%	High
	Average Behavior	**70%**	**65%**	**5 %**	**Med**

Behaviors

The percentage of O2 responses in the "Strongly Agree" category by the treatment group with respect to identity theft preventive behaviors was 4.7% higher than it was in the comparison group. One exception was Item 8B re: securing out-going mail. For this item, the percentage of responses in the "Strongly Agree" category was 22% higher in the comparison group than it was in the treatment group.

With respect to Item 10B, (not carrying a social security card) the treatment group showed the greatest difference when compared to the comparison group. For this item, the percentage of O2 responses in the "Strongly Agree" category was 39% higher than it was in the comparison group.

5.5 Analysis of Change

5.5.1 Treatment Group

An analysis of the changes that occurred in the treatment group, after the training intervention, as measured by O2 responses, is presented in this section. Table 21 presents the comparison between responses in the "Strongly Agree" category for the two surveys (O1 and O2). Overall, with respect to attitudes, the percentage of O2 responses in the "Strongly Agree" category increased by 16% and with respect to behaviors the percentage of O2 responses in the "Strongly Agree" category increased by 37%.

Attitudes

The treatment group reported low to medium increases in six of the ten attitude-related items. However, greater increases in positive attitudes occurred with respect to destroying credit card receipts, destroying old personal correspondence, destroying old utility bills and placing out-going mail in a secure mailbox. The specific changes in attitudes were as follows:

- Credit card receipts: Prior to training, 78% of the participants strongly agreed that old credit card receipts should be destroyed; after intervention 96% of the participants strongly agreed that old credit card receipts should be destroyed. This was a 23% increase after the training.

- Old personal correspondence: Prior to training, 35% of the participants strongly agreed that old personal correspondence should be destroyed; after intervention, 61% of the participants strongly agreed that old personal correspondence should be destroyed. This was a 74% increase after the training.

- Old utility bills: While prior to training 48% of the participants strongly agreed that old utility bills should be destroyed, after intervention 61% of the participants strongly agreed that old utility bills should be destroyed. This was a 27% increase after the training.

- Secure out-going mail: While prior to training 61% of the participants strongly agreed that securing out-going mail should be performed, after intervention 74% of the participants strongly agreed that securing out-going mail should be performed. This was a 21% increase after the training.

Table 21.

Treatment Group: Analysis of Change (TO1 & TO2)

		TO1	TO2	% Change	
	Attitude	**Strongly Agree**	**Strongly Agree**		
1A	Should destroy bank statements	74%	83%	+ 12%	Med
2A	Should destroy credit card receipts	78%	96%	+ 23%	High
3A	Should destroy pre-approved credit card offers	87%	96%	+ 10%	Med
4A	Should destroy old personal correspondence	35%	61%	+ 74%	High
5A	Should destroy pay stubs	65%	70%	+ 8%	Low
6A	Should destroy old utility bills	48%	61%	+ 27%	High
7A	Should not reveal social security number	83%	83%	0%	Low
8A	Should place out-going mail in mailbox	61%	74%	+ 21%	High
9A	Should not give out contact information	78%	87%	+ 12%	Med
10A	Should not carry my social security card	70%	78%	+ 11%	Med
	Average Attitude	**68%**	**79%**	**+ 16%**	**Med**
	Behavior				
1B	Destroy bank statements	48%	59%	+ 23%	High
2B	Destroy credit card receipts	61%	70%	+ 15%	Med
3B	Destroy pre-approved credit card offers	83%	87%	+ 5%	Low
4B	Destroy old personal correspondence	26%	48%	+ 85%	High
5B	Destroy pay stubs	43%	57%	+ 33%	High
6B	Destroy old utility bills	43%	52%	+ 21%	High
7B	Do not reveal social security number	87%	91%	+ 5%	Low
8B	Place out-going mail in secure mailbox	30%	57%	+ 90%	High
9B	Do not give out contact information	52%	96%	+ 85%	High
10B	Do not carry my social security card	40%	83%	+ 108%	High
	Average Behavior	**51%**	**70%**	**+ 37%**	**High**

Behaviors

The treatment group reported an overall increase of 37% in the use of identity theft preventive behaviors, with the greatest changes in behavior reported for seven of the ten items. In particular, there were increases in behaviors relating to: destroying bank statements, placing out-going mail in secure mailboxes, destroying old personal correspondence, not revealing contact information to strangers and not carrying social security cards. The specific changes in behavior were as follows:

- Bank statements: In the O1 survey, 48% of the participants reported that they destroyed old bank statements; after intervention 59% reported doing so.. This was a 23% increase after the training.

- Old personal correspondence: In the O1 survey 26% of the participants reported that they destroyed old personal correspondence; after intervention, 48% reported doing so. This was an 85% increase after the training.

- Old pay stubs: In the O1 survey, 26% of the participants reported destroying their pay stubs; after intervention, 48% reported doing so. This was a 33% increase after the training.

- Old utility bills: In the O1 survey, 43% of the participants reported destroying their utility bills; after intervention, 52% reported doing so behavior. This was a 21% increase after the training.

- Secure out-going mail: In the O1 survey, 30% of the participants reported that they placed out-going mail in a secure mailbox; after intervention, 57% reported doing so. This was a 90% increase after the training.

- Personal contact information: In the O1 survey, 52% of the participants reported that they did not reveal their contact information to strangers; after intervention, 96% reported not doing so. This was an 85% increase after the training.

- Social security cards: In the O1 survey, 40% of the participants reported not carrying their social security cards in their wallets; after intervention, 83% reported not doing so. This was a 108% increase after the training.

5.5.2 Comparison Group

Table 22 presents an analysis of any changes that occurred in the comparison group as measured by the O2 survey. Overall, in the comparison group, attitudes towards identity theft prevention techniques were almost identical (3% decrease); however, positive behaviors increased by 10%.

Attitudes

The percentage of O2 responses in the "Strongly Agree" category reported by the comparison group participants, with respect to attitudes, decreased in seven of the ten items. The greatest decreases were reported with respect to destroying pre-approved credit cards (-13%), destroying old personal correspondence (-14%), and destroying old utility bills (-18%). However, increases in positive attitudes of 15% were reported for two items: destroying credit card receipts and placing out-going mail in a secure mail-box. Attitudes towards not revealing social security numbers remained unchanged.

Behaviors

Overall, with respect to behaviors, the percentage of O2 responses in the "Strongly Agree" category reported by the comparison group participants, increased by 10%. Behaviors related to destroying pre-approved credit card offers and not revealing a social security number remained the same, at 74% and 82% respectively. The greatest changes in behavior reported by the comparison group participants concerned destroying credit card receipts, destroying pay stubs, and not carrying social security cards.

The specific changes were as follows:

- Credit card receipts: In the O1 survey, 62% of the participants reported destroying credit cards receipts; 74% reported doing so two weeks later. This was a 19% increase, without the benefit of training.

- Old pay stubs: In the O1 survey, 43% of the participants reported destroying pay stubs; 56% reported doing so two weeks later. This was a 30% increase, without the benefit of training.

- Secure out-going mail: In the O1 first survey, 68% of the participants reported placing out-going mail in secure mailbox, 79% reported doing so two weeks later. This was a 16% increase, without the benefit of training.

- Carrying security card: In the O1 survey 32% of the participants reported not carrying a social security card; 44% reported not doing so two weeks later. This was a 38% increase, without the benefit of training.

Table 22.
Comparison Group: Analysis of Change (CO1 vs. CO2)

		CO1	CO2	% Change	
	Attitude	**Strongly Agree**	**Strongly Agree**		
1A	Should destroy bank statements	74%	71%	- 4%	Low
2A	Should destroy credit card receipts	79%	91%	+ 15%	Med
3A	Should destroy pre-approved credit card offers	94%	82%	- 13%	Med
4A	Should destroy old personal correspondence.	79%	68%	- 14%	Med
5A	Should destroy pay stubs	71%	70%	- 1%	Low
6A	Should destroy old utility bills	68%	56%	- 18%	Med
7A	Should not reveal social security number	79%	79%	0%	None
8A	Should place out-going mail in mailbox	71%	82%	+ 15%	Med
9A	Should not give out contact information	79%	74%	- 6%	Low
10A	Should not carry my social security card	56%	53%	- 5%	Low
	Average Attitude	**75%**	**73%**	**- 3%**	**Low**
	Behavior				
1B	Destroy bank statements	62%	59%	- 5%	Low
2B	Destroy credit card receipts	62%	74%	+ 19%	Med
3B	Destroy pre-approved credit card offers	74%	74%	0%	None
4B	Destroy old personal correspondence	47%	53%	+ 13%	Low
5B	Destroy pay stubs	43%	56%	+ 30%	High
6B	Destroy old utility bills	45%	50%	+ 10%	Low
7B	Do not reveal social security number	82%	82%	+ 0%	None
8B	Place out-going mail in secure mailbox	68%	79%	+ 16%	Med
9B	Do not give out contact information	74%	82%	+ 11%	Low
10B	Do not carry my social security card	32%	44%	+ 38%	High
	Average Behavior	**59%**	**65%**	**+ 10%**	**Med**

5.5.3 Between Group Analysis of Change

Table 23 presents a comparison of the O1- O2 changes in the treatment and comparison groups. With respect to attitudes, the amount of change in the treatment group exceeded that in the comparison group by 19%. With respect to behaviors, the amount of change in the treatment group exceeded that in the comparison group by 27%.

Attitudes

The treatment group exceeded the comparison group in O1-O2 changes reported, with respect to all items except one: Item 7A, " not revealing social security numbers". For this item there was 0 % difference between the groups; in fact, for this item, no change was reported for either group.

The greatest differences in the amount of change reported by the two groups, with respect to attitudes, occurred with two items: destroying old personal correspondence (88%) and destroying old utility bills (45%). The differences between the two groups were as follows:

- Credit Card Offers: While the treatment group showed an increase in positive attitudes toward destroying pre-approved credit card offers of 10%, the comparison group reported a decrease of 13% during the same time period. The O1-O2 change in the treatment group exceeded the comparison group by 23%. .

- Old Personal Correspondence: While the treatment group showed an increase of 74% in positive attitudes toward destroying old personal correspondence, the comparison group reported a decrease of 14% during the same time period. The O1-O2 change in the treatment group exceeded the comparison group by 88%.

- Old Utility bills: While the treatment group showed an increase of 27% in positive attitudes toward destroying old utility bills, the comparison group reported a decrease of 18% during the same period. The 01-02 change in the

treatment group exceeded the comparison group by 45%.

Table 23.
Between Group Analysis of Change

		Comparison	Treatment	Difference	
	Attitude	**% Change**	**% Change**		
1A	Should destroy bank statements	- 4%	+ 12%	+ 16%	Med
2A	Should destroy credit card receipts	+ 15%	+ 23%	+ 8%	Low
3A	Should destroy pre-approved credit card offers	- 13%	+ 10%	+ 23%	High
4A	Should destroy old personal correspondence	- 14%	+ 74%	+ 88%	High
5A	Should destroy pay stubs	- 1%	+ 8%	+ 9%	Low
6A	Should destroy old utility bills	- 18%	+ 27%	+ 45%	High
7A	Should not reveal social security number	0%	0%	0%	None
8A	Should place out-going mail in mailbox	+ 15%	+ 21%	+ 6%	Low
9A	Should not give out contact information	- 6%	+ 12%	+ 18%	Med
10A	Should carry my social security card	+ 5%	+ 11%	+ 16%	Med
	Average Attitude	**- 3%**	**+ 16%**	**+ 19%**	**Med**
	Behavior				
1B	Destroy bank statements	- 5%	+ 23%	+ 28%	High
2B	Destroy credit card receipts	+ 19%	+ 15%	- 4%	Low
3B	Destroy pre-approved credit card offers	0%	+ 5%	+ 5%	Low
4B	Destroy old personal correspondence	+ 13%	+ 85%	+ 98%	High
5B	Destroy pay stubs	+ 30%	+ 33%	+ 3%	Low
6B	Destroy old utility bills	+ 10%	+ 21%	+ 11%	Med
7B	Do not reveal social security number	+ 0%	+ 5%	+ 5	Low
8B	Place out-going mail in secure mailbox	+ 16%	+ 90%	74%	High
9B	Do not give out contact information	+ 11%	+ 85%	+ 74%	High
10B	Do not carry my social security card	+ 38%	+ 108%	+ 70%	High
	Average Behavior	**+ 10%**	**+ 37%**	**+ 27%**	**High**

Behavior

The greatest differences between the groups ,in the amount of O1-O2 behavioral change, concerned the following items (for which the treatment group exceeded the comparison group): destroying old personal correspondence (98%); securing out-going mail, (74%); giving out personal contract information (74%), not carrying social security cards (70%), and destroying bank statements (28%).

However, with respect to one item, destroying credit card receipts, the amount of O1-O2 change in the comparison group exceeded that of the treatment group by 4 %.

5.6 Additional Measures of Change

5.6.1 Ordering a Credit Report

During the interview process, participants in both groups were asked whether they had ordered a credit report during the time period between the O1 and O2 surveys. In the treatment group, 17% of the participants reported having done so, as compared to 6% of the comparison group participants. As shown in Table 24, this was a 300% increase by the treatment group in the use of this identity theft preventive technique, as compared to a 6% increase for the comparison group.

Table 24.
Credit Reports Ordered

		Observation 1		Observation 2		
Group	Sample Size	Reports Ordered @ O1	Percentage	Reports Ordered @ O2	Percentage	% Increase
Treatment Group	23	1	4%	4	17%	300%
Comparison Group	34	0	0%	2	6%	N/A

5.6.2 Influencing Factors- Time Devoted to Topic

Both the FTC and the USPS recognize all the preventive techniques taught in the CASE program as being critical to reducing the incidence of identity theft. However, the amount of time devoted to each topic varied during the training seminar. Therefore, the researcher conducted an analysis of the time devoted to each topic area in order to assess how this factor influenced the effect of the training on the treatment group, as measured by the amount of O1-O2 change.

As shown in Table 25, the greatest amount of time was devoted to Items 7-10; moreover, the changes in behavior associated with three of those four items (Items 8, 9 and 10, re: out-going mail, contact information and carrying social security card, reflected the greatest impact of the training on the participants with the amount of change reported as 90%, 85%, and 108% respectively. Thus, the data showed that the amount of time devoted to a specific topic or content area in the training had a direct influence on the level of adoption of the behavior. However, with respect to attitude change, this relationship was not demonstrated.

Table 25.
Comparison of Time Devoted and Level of Change

	Dependent Variable	Time Spent on Topic (Min)	% Change Attitude	% Change Behavior
1	Should destroy bank statements	2	+ 12%	+ 23%
2	Should destroy credit card receipts	4	+ 23%	+ 13%
3	Should destroy pre-approved credit card offers	2	+ 10%	+ 5%
4	Should destroy old personal correspondence.	1	+ 74%	+ 85%
5	Should destroy pay stubs	1	+ 8%	+ 33%
6	Should destroy old utility bills	1	+ 27%	+ 21%
7	Should not reveal social security number	10	0%	+ 5%
8	Should place out-going mail in mailbox	10	+ 21%	+ 90%
9	Should not give out contact information	8	+ 12%	+ 85%
10	Should not carry my social security card	10	+ 11%	+ 108%
	Ordered credit report	1	**N/A**	**17%**

5.6.3 Influencing Factors- Demographic Characteristic: Gender

This section examines how gender influenced the effect of the training on the

treatment group, as measured by the amount of O1-O2 change. As mentioned previously,

both the treatment and comparison groups were predominantly female. For analysis, the

treatment group was divided into two categories: male and female.

As shown in Table 26, the O1-O2 positive attitude change toward identity theft

preventive techniques among females exceeded that among males by 9%. With regard to

destroying old personal correspondence, females exceeded males by 177%. On the other

hand, with respect to three items, the O1-O2 change was greater among males than

females. These were: destroying pre-approved credit card offers (23%), destroying pay

stubs (44%), and destroying old utility bills (21%).

As shown in Table 26, females also exceeded males, by 7% overall, with respect to

O1-O2 positive behavioral change. The greatest differences between the genders were

reported for the following four items: destroying credit card receipts, for which females

exceeded males by 58%; destroying old personal correspondence for which females

exceeded males by 23%; destroying old utility bills for which females exceeded males by

23% and not revealing social security numbers for which females exceeded males by 20%.

However, with respect to two behavior items, the O1-O2 positive change was

greater among males than females. Males exceeded females by 60% with respect to

placing out-going mail in a secure mailbox and by 34% with respect to not carrying a social

security card.

Table 26.
Demographic Influence: Gender

	Attitude	Male Strongly Agree % Change	Female Strongly Agree % Change	Between Group Difference	
1A	Should destroy bank statements	+ 29 %	+ 15 %	14 %	Med
2A	Should destroy credit card receipts	+ 18 %	+ 32 %	14 %	Med
3A	Should destroy pre-approved credit card offers	+ 29 %	+ 6 %	23 %	High
4A	Should destroy old personal correspondence	- 77 %	+ 100 %	177 %	High
5A	Should destroy pay stubs	+ 44 %	0 %	44 %	High
6A	Should destroy old utility bills	+ 44 %	+ 23 %	21 %	High
7A	Should not reveal social security number	0 %	- 7 %	7 %	Low
8A	Should place out-going mail in mailbox	0 %	+ 17 %	17 %	Med
9A	Should not give out contact information	0 %	+ 17 %	17 %	Med
10A	Should not carry my social security card	+ 29 %	+ 10 %	19 %	Med
	Average Attitude	**+ 12%**	**+ 21 %**	**9 %**	**Low**
	Behavior				
1B	Destroy bank statements	0 %	+ 12 %	12 %	Med
2B	Destroy credit card receipts	- 31 %	+ 27 %	58 %	High
3B	Destroy pre-approved credit card offers	0 %	+ 7 %	7 %	Low
4B	Destroy old personal correspondence	0 %	+ 23 %	23 %	High
5B	Destroy pay stubs	0 %	+ 12 %	12 %	Med
6B	Destroy old utility bills	0 %	+ 23 %	23 %	High
7B	Do not reveal social security number	- 5 %	+ 15 %	20 %	High
8B	Place out-going mail in secure mailbox	+ 125 %	+ 65 %	60 %	High
9B	Do not give out contact information	+ 24 %	+ 32 %	8 %	Low
10B	Do not carry my social security card	+ 53 %	+ 19 %	34 %	High
	Average Behavior	**+ 17 %**	**+ 24 %**	**7 %**	**Low**

5.6.4 Influencing Factors- Demographic Characteristic: Income

This section examines how income level influenced the effect of the training on the treatment group, as measured by the amount of O1-O2 change. For analysis, the treatment group was divided into two categories: those participants earning more than $50K and those earning $50 K or less. .

As shown in Table 27, the O1-O2 change in positive attitudes reported by participants earning greater than $50K exceeded that reported by the lower income participants, by 23%. The differences were greatest with respect to the following four items: destroying bank statements (42%), destroying old personal correspondence (116%), destroying old pay stubs (21%), destroying old utility bills (27%), and not carrying a social security card (27%).

As shown in Table 27, with respect to the O1-O2 change in behaviors, the results in the two income categories were reversed. Here, the lower income group exceeded the higher income group by 14% overall in positive behavioral change. The differences between the two sub-groups were greatest with respect to the following four items: destroying bank statements (27%), destroying old pay stubs (57%), not giving out contact information (60%), and not carrying a social security card (42%).

One exception occurred with respect to placing out-going mail in a secure mailbox. For this item, the O1-O2 positive change reported by the higher income group exceeded that of the lower income group by 75%.

Table 27.

Demographic Influence: Income

		Income > 50K Strongly Agree	Income < 50K Strongly Agree	Between Group Difference	
	Attitude	**% Change**	**% Change**		
1A	Should destroy bank statements	+ 27 %	- 15 %	42 %	High
2A	Should destroy credit card receipts	+ 25 %	+ 15 %	10 %	Med
3A	Should destroy pre-approved credit card offers	0 %	+ 17 %	17 %	Med
4A	Should destroy old personal correspondence.	+ 16 %9	+ 53 %	116 %	High
5A	Should destroy pay stubs	+ 8 %	+ 29 %	21 %	High
6A	Should destroy old utility bills	- 27 %	0 %	27 %	High
7A	Should not reveal social security number	- 7 %	- 15 %	8 %	Low
8A	Should place out-going mail in mailbox	+ 37 %	- 15 %	17 %	Med
9A	Should not give out contact information	+ 27 %	- 13 %	14 %	Med
10A	Should not carry my social security card	+ 27 %	0 %	27 %	High
	Average Attitude	**+ 29 %**	**+ 6 %**	**+ 23 %**	**High**
	Behavior				
1B	Destroy bank statements	- 13 %	24 %	27%	High
2B	Destroy credit card receipts	+ 23 %	0 %	23%	High
3B	Destroy pre-approved credit card offers	- 10 %	0 %	10%	Med
4B	Destroy old personal correspondence	62 %	+ 69 %	7%	Low
5B	Destroy pay stubs	+ 43 %	+100 %	57%	High
6B	Destroy old utility bills	+ 18 %	+ 18 %	0%	Low
7B	Do not reveal social security number	0 %	+ 17 %	17%	Med
8B	Place out-going mail in secure mailbox	+ 106 %	+ 31 %	75%	High
9B	Do not give out contact information	+ 7 %	+ 67 %	60%	High
10B	Do not carry my social security card	27 %	+ 69 %	42%	High
	Average Behavior	**26%**	**40%**	**14 %**	**Med**

5.6.5 Influencing Factors- Demographic Characteristic: Marital Status

This section examines how marital status influenced the effect of the training on the treatment group, as measured by the amount of O1-O2 change. For analysis, the treatment group was divided into two categories: married and non-married.

As shown in Table 28, the married treatment group participants showed a greater amount of O1-O2 positive change in attitudes, by 14%, as compared to the non-married participants. The greatest differences in the degree of change were reported with respect to the following five items: destroying credit card receipts (99%), destroying old personal correspondence (116%), destroying old utility bills (53%), placing out-going mail in a secure mailbox (52%), and not giving out contact information (56%).

With respect to behaviors, married participants also exceeded those who were unmarried in the amount of O1-O2 positive change reported. As shown in Table 28, the overall difference was 16%. The greatest differences were reported with respect to the following four items: destroying old personal correspondence (91%), destroying old pay stubs (38%), placing outgoing mail in a secure mailbox (102%) and not carrying a social security card (39%).

Table 28.

Demographic Influence: Marital Status

		Married Strongly Agree	Not-married Strongly Agree	Between Group Difference	
	Attitude	**% Change**	**% Change**		
1A	Should destroy bank statements	19 %	0 %	19 %	Med
2A	Should destroy credit card receipts	7 %	106 %	99 %	High
3A	Should destroy pre-approved credit card offers	7 %	17 %	10 %	Med
4A	Should destroy old personal correspondence.	169 %	53 %	116 %	High
5A	Should destroy pay stubs	13 %	0 %	13 %	Med
6A	Should destroy old utility bills	0 %	53 %	53 %	High
7A	Should not reveal social security number	0 %	-23 %	23 %	High
8A	Should place out-going mail in mailbox	37 %	-15 %	52 %	High
9A	Should not give out contact information	56 %	0 %	56 %	High
10A	Should not carry my social security card	19 %	0 %	19 %	Med
	Average Attitude	**33%**	**19%**	**14%**	**Med**
	Behavior				
1B	Destroy bank statements	0 %	18 %	18 %	Med
2B	Destroy credit card receipts	11 %	13 %	2 %	Low
3B	Destroy pre-approved credit card offers	0 %	17 %	17 %	Med
4B	Destroy old personal correspondence	144 %	53 %	91 %	High
5B	Destroy pay stubs	15 %	53 %	38 %	High
6B	Destroy old utility bills	18 %	18 %	0 %	Low
7B	Do not reveal social security number	7 %	0 %	7 %	Low
8B	Place out-going mail in secure mailbox	131 %	29 %	102 %	High
9B	Do not give out contact information	14 %	15 %	1 %	Low
10B	Do not carry my social security card	39 %	0 %	39 %	High
	Average Behavior	**38 %**	**22 %**	**16 %**	**Med**

5.6.6 Influencing Factors- Demographic Characteristic: Education

This section examines how education level influenced the effect of the training on the treatment group, as measured by the amount of O1-O2 change. For analysis, the treatment group was divided into two categories: those participants who reported having earned at least a baccalaureate degree, and those who reported no college education.

As shown in Table 29, the amount of O1-O2 change in positive attitudes toward identity theft preventive techniques reported by participants without a college education exceeded that reported by the college graduates, by 9% overall. Furthermore, the greatest differences between the two subgroups in attitude change, was exhibited with respect to two items: destroying pre-approved credit card offers (42%) and not carrying a social security card (76%).

As shown in Table 29, with respect to the amount of O1-O2 change in behaviors, the results in the two educational categories were reversed. Here, the college graduates exceeded the non-degree holders by 14% overall in positive behaviors. The greatest difference in behavioral change between the two sub-groups, was reported with respect to the following three items: destroying credit card receipts (56%), destroying old personal correspondence (100%), and not giving out contact information (59%).

Table 29.

Demographic Influence: Education

		College Strongly Agree	No College Strongly Agree	Between Group Difference	
	Attitude	**% Change**	**% Change**		
1A	Should destroy bank statements	+ 27 %	- 3 %	30 %	High
2A	Should destroy credit card receipts	+ 35 %	0 %	35 %	High
3A	Should destroy pre-approved credit card offers	+ 17 %	+ 59 %	42 %	High
4A	Should destroy old personal correspondence.	+ 101 %	+ 100 %	1 %	Low
5A	Should destroy pay stubs	0 %	+ 30 %	30 %	High
6A	Should destroy old utility bills	+ 23 %	0 %	23%	High
7A	Should not reveal social security number	- 8 %	0 %	8%	Low
8A	Should place out-going mail in mailbox	+ 10 %	+ 18 %	8%	Low
9A	Should not give out contact information	0 %	+ 35 %	35%	High
10A	Should not carry my social security card	0 %	+ 76 %	76%	High
	Average Attitude	**+ 21 %**	**+ 32 %**	**11%**	**Med**
	Behavior				
1B	Destroy bank statements	+ 50 %	41 %	9 %	Low
2B	Destroy credit card receipts	+ 33 %	-23 %	56 %	High
3B	Destroy pre-approved credit card offers	+ 10 %	-14 %	24 %	High
4B	Destroy old personal correspondence	+ 131 %	+ 31 %	100 %	High
5B	Destroy pay stubs	+ 35 %	+ 29 %	6 %	Low
6B	Destroy old utility bills	0 %	+ 0 %	0 %	Low
7B	Do not reveal social security number	0 %	+ 15 %	15 %	Med
8B	Place out-going mail in secure mailbox	+ 77 %	+ 44 %	33 %	High
9B	Do not give out contact information	+ 0 %	+ 59 %	59 %	High
10B	Do not carry my social security card	+ 21 %	+ 36 %	15 %	Med
	Average Behavior	**+ 36 %**	**+ 22 %**	**14 %**	**Med**

5.6.7 Influencing Factors- Demographic Characteristic: Race

This section examines how race influenced the effect of the training on the treatment group, as measured by the amount of O1-O2 change. For analysis, the treatment group was divided into two categories: Caucasian and Other.

As shown in Table 30, Caucasian participants reported a greater degree of O1-O2 change in positive attitudes toward identity theft preventive techniques by 21%, as compared to the participants of other races. The differences between the two subgroups were the greatest with respect to three items: destroying old bank statements (50%), destroying old personal correspondence (116%) and old utility bills (30%).

As shown in Table 30, with respect to behaviors, Caucasian participants also reported a greater degree of O1-O2 positive change, by 11%. The greatest differences between the two sub-groups were reported with respect to the following five items: destroying bank statements (29%), destroying old personal correspondence (91%), destroying old utility bills (53%), placing out-going mail in a secure mailbox (47%), and not carrying a social security card (46%).

Table 30.
Demographic Influence: Race

		Caucasian Strongly Agree	Other Strongly Agree	Between Group Difference	
	Attitude	**% Change**	**% Change**		
1A	Should destroy bank statements	- 65 %	- 15 %	50 %	High
2A	Should destroy credit card receipts	+ 14 %	+ 36 %	22 %	High
3A	Should destroy pre-approved credit card offers	+ 17 %	0 %	17 %	Med
4A	Should destroy old personal correspondence	+ 169 %	+ 53 %	116 %	High
5A	Should destroy pay stubs	+ 12 %	0 %	12 %	Med
6A	Should destroy old utility bills	+ 30 %	0 %	30 %	High
7A	Should not reveal social security number	0 %	- 13 %	13 %	Med
8A	Should place out-going mail in mailbox	+ 43 %	- 13 %	13 %	Med
9A	Should not give out contact information	+ 27 %	- 13 %	14 %	Med
10A	Should not carry my social security card	+ 3 %	0 %	3 %	Low
	Average Attitude	**+ 25%**	**+ 4%**	**21 %**	**High**
	Behavior				
1B	Destroy bank statements	0 %	+ 29 %	29 %	High
2B	Destroy credit card receipts	+ 13 %	+ 18 %	5 %	Low
3B	Destroy pre-approved credit card offers	0 %	+ 17 %	17 %	Med
4B	Destroy old personal correspondence	+ 144 %	+ 53 %	91 %	High
5B	Destroy pay stubs	+ 36 %	+ 18 %	18 %	Med
6B	Destroy old utility bills	0 %	+ 53 %	53 %	High
7B	Do not reveal social security number	+ 7 %	- 26 %	19 %	Med
8B	Place out-going mail in secure mailbox	+ 100 %	+ 53 %	47 %	High
9B	Do not give out contact information	+ 17 %	+ 35 %	18 %	Med
10B	Do not carry my social security card	+ 46 %	0 %	46 %	High
	Average Behavior	**+ 36 %**	**+ 25 %**	**11 %**	**Med**

5.6.8 Influencing Factors- Demographic Characteristic: Internet Access

This section examines how access to the Internet influenced the effect of the training on the treatment group, as measured by the amount of O1-O2 change. For analysis, the treatment group was divided into two categories: those with Internet access and those without.

As shown in Table 31, participants who had access to the Internet showed a greater positive change in attitudes toward identity theft preventive techniques by 24% , as compared to those without internet access. In fact, overall, the amount of O1-O2 change in attitudes reported by the those without Internet access actually decreased by 6%.

The greatest difference between the two sub-groups was reported with respect to: destroying old personal correspondence (122%), not revealing a social security number (59%), placing outgoing mail in a secure mailbox (43%), and not giving out contact information (54%).

As shown in Table 31, the amount of O1-O2 change in behaviors reported by participants who had Internet access also exceeded that reported by those without such access; with respect to behaviors, the difference was 58%. The greatest differences were reported for the following five items: destroying old personal correspondence (169%), destroying old utility bills (74%), not revealing a social security number (267%), placing out-going mail in a secure mailbox (95%), and not giving out contact information (83%).

Table 31.
Demographic Influence: Internet Access

		Yes Strongly Agree	No Strongly Agree	Between Group Difference	
	Attitude	**% Change**	**% Change**		
1A	Should destroy bank statements	+ 23 %	- 24 %	1 %	Low
2A	Should destroy credit card receipts	+ 28 %	0 %	28 %	High
3A	Should destroy pre-approved credit card offers	+ 11 %	0 %	11 %	Med
4A	Should destroy old personal correspondence	+ 153 %	+ 31 %	122 %	High
5A	Should destroy pay stubs	+ 10 %	0 %	10 %	Low
6A	Should destroy old utility bills	+ 23 %	0 %	23 %	High
7A	Should not reveal social security number	- 59 %	0 %	59 %	High
8A	Should place out-going mail in mailbox	+ 27 %	- 70 %	43 %	High
9A	Should not give out contact information	- 54 %	0 %	54 %	High
10A	Should not carry my social security card	+ 14 %	0 %	14 %	Med
	Average Attitude	**+ 18%**	**- 6 %**	**24 %**	**High**
	Behavior				
1B	Destroy bank statements	+ 11 %	0 %	11 %	Med
2B	Destroy credit card receipts	0 %	- 24 %	24 %	High
3B	Destroy pre-approved credit card offers	+ 15 %	0 %	15 %	Med
4B	Destroy old personal correspondence	+ 169 %	0 %	169 %	High
5B	Destroy pay stubs	+ 23 %	+ 44 %	21 %	High
6B	Destroy old utility bills	+ 43 %	- 31 %	74 %	High
7B	Do not reveal social security number	+ 236 %	- 31 %	267 %	High
8B	Place out-going mail in secure mailbox	+ 95 %	0 %	95 %	High
9B	Do not give out contact information	+ 5 %	+ 89 %	83 %	High
10B	Do not carry my social security card	+ 29 %	0 %	29 %	High
	Average Behavior	**+ 63%**	**+5%**	**58 %**	**High**

Chapter 6

Research Results

This chapter examines the degree of support found for the research questions posed in Chapter 3. In addition, it describes the findings derived from the analysis of the data, including post-intervention effects on the treatment group; between group comparisons of changes; the influences of demographic characteristics on the results; and an analysis of factors affecting results in the comparison group.

6.1 Post-Intervention Effects on Treatment Group

The first two research questions of this study were:

1. Is there a relationship between participation in the CASE training program and attitudes towards identity theft prevention?

2. Is there a relationship between participation in the CASE training program and the use of identity theft prevention behaviors?

The findings of this study suggest that the CASE training program influenced both the attitudes and behaviors of seniors towards identity theft prevention techniques. As shown in Table 21, positive changes in attitudes and behaviors occurred in the treatment group, as a result of the training. Levels of change classified as "High", occurred in four of the ten attitude items, with an overall change of 16%. Positive changes in the attitude items, as a result of the intervention, ranged from increases of 8% to 27%.

With respect to attitudes, no change occurred with respect to Item 7A, revealing social security numbers; however, this item was reported positively by 83% of the treatment group participants at both O1 and O2, indicating that there already was a high awareness of the importance of this particular identity theft prevention technique.

With respect to behavior, levels of change classified as "High" occurred in seven of the ten items, with an overall increase of 37%. Changes in the behaviors as a result of the intervention ranged from increases of 5% to 108%. The most significant changes occurred in the behaviors of destroying old personal correspondence (Item 4B-85%), placing outgoing mail in a secure mailbox (Item8B-90%), not giving out contact information (Item 9B-85%), and not carrying a social security card (Item 10B- 108%).

As shown in Table 25, three of these items (8B, 9B, and 10B) were given significant coverage in the training session. This helps to explain the significant positive changes in behavior that occurred with respect to these particular items. However, the high degree of change reported in Item 4B cannot be explained based on its coverage in the training; nor was it explored in follow-up interviews. It is plausible that as a result of the emphasis placed on destroying correspondence of various types (e.g. old bills, credit card papers, etc.) that the seniors interpreted this as personal correspondence and acted accordingly.

6.2 Between Group Comparisons of Change

The first two research questions are further supported by the examination of the between group comparison of changes.

Table 23 shows the differences in the level of O1-O2 change that occurred in the treatment and comparison groups. Overall, the treatment group reported a 19% greater increase in positive attitudes as compared to the comparison group. The greatest difference in attitudes between the two groups occurred with respect to destroying old personal correspondence (88%) and destroying old utility bills (45%). These differences are consistent with the high level of overall change reported by the treatment group.

The fact that no change occurred with respect to revealing social security numbers in either group, suggested that seniors already recognized the importance of protecting this information. This is supported by the data, where a high percentage of the sample (83% of the treatment group and 79% of the comparison group) reported positively on this item in both O1 and O2.

Not surprisingly, the greatest difference in the amount of behavior change between the groups occurred with respect to the same four items (Items 4B, 8B, 9B, and 10B) for which the treatment group reported the greatest change in behavior. Overall, the treatment group reported a 27% greater change in behaviors than did the comparison group, suggesting the positive influence the training intervention had on the behaviors of the seniors.

The third and final research question posed by this dissertation was:

3. Is there a relationship between participation in CASE training program and the practice of ordering a credit report?

Ordering a credit report is one of the most significant techniques for identity theft prevention. As shown in Table 24, the number of treatment group participants who ordered a credit report after the intervention increased by 300% as compared to 6% in the comparison group. The data suggested, therefore, that the training had a significant impact on the behavior of ordering a credit report.

6.3 Influences of Demographic Characteristics

While these findings suggested support for the three research questions posed by this study, the researcher also evaluated the effects of certain demographic characteristics to determine if they may have had a contributing influence on the observed changes.

As can be seen in the demographic analysis presented in Chapter 5, the treatment group was skewed in its representation of certain demographic characteristics reported.

Tables 32 and 33 summarize the predominant demographic characteristics of the treatment group.

Table 32.
Predominant Demographic Characteristics

Gender		Income		Marital Status	
Male	26.1%	< $50K	34.7%	Married	65.2%
Female	73.9%	> $50K	65.2%	Other	34.8%

Table 33.
Predominant Demographic Characteristics

Education		Race		Internet Access	
No college	34.8%	Caucasian	65.2%	Yes	82.6%
College	65.1%	Other	34.7%	No	17.4%

The data analysis indicated that the only demographic characteristic to show a strong relationship with the degree of change in both attitudes and behaviors was access to the Internet. Participants who had such access exhibited a 24% greater change in attitudes and a 59% greater change in behaviors than did those without internet access.

Other demographic characteristics that were found to have some influence on changes in attitude were income (22%) and race (21%). However, it was not determined whether a relationship existed between income and race. With respect to gender, although the results for the males and females were not significantly different, the females did show greater change. These results were consistent with literature which suggests that females are more concerned about threats to personal privacy than are males (Acherman, Cranor, & Reagle, 1999).

The findings of this research, with respect to the influence of income on identity theft prevention behaviors, conflict with previous research which suggested that wealthier seniors were more concerned about identity theft (O'Neill & Xiao, 2004).

6.4 Unexpected Comparison Group Findings

It was anticipated that there would be little if any change in attitudes and behaviors among comparison group participants, since they did not have the benefit of the training. While this expectation was fulfilled with respect to changes in attitudes, the comparison group reported an unexpected increase of 10% change in behaviors.

Initially, it was considered that the survey itself might have triggered this change; however, if that were the case, a similar change should have occurred with respect to attitudes. Therefore, the researcher examined other influencing factors more closely.

One plausible alternative explanation for the behavioral change by the comparison group, relates to a computer theft in which data stored by the Veteran's Administration (First Gov.gov, 2006) was kept. This incident, which occurred during the period of the study, received a great deal of media coverage in the Washington D.C. area.

In the follow-up interviews, the comparison group participants were asked about their awareness of the crime and about their concern for their personal information as a result of this crime. Twenty four participants (71%) reported that they were highly concerned about the event.

Considering all the media coverage that took place, this event had the potential to affect the treatment group as well. However, 50% of the treatment group participants interviewed reported that the event did not cause them significant concern. The researcher believes that the VA theft and its aftermath provide a plausible explanation for the unexpected behavioral changes by the comparison group.

Chapter 7

Implications of Results

7.1 Contribution to Knowledge

Limited research exists with respect to the relationship between identity theft training programs and their impact on the attitudes and behaviors of consumers. Even fewer studies have been conducted on the prevention of identity theft crimes against senior citizens. This study provided an investigation of the impact of the CASE Training Model on the attitudes and behaviors of senior citizens.

A significant contribution of this research was to provide validity for the previous work done by McKenna and Miller (2003), which examined the effectiveness of the CASE model. Their research evaluated the impact of the training on the participants through the analysis of post-training self-reports by participants in which they were asked to assess their attitudes and behaviors before and after training.

This dissertation furthered McKenna and Miller's work by utilizing:

1. A pre-test and post-test design to provide a means by which the amount of change could be measured in the treatment group.

2. A comparison group which did not experience the intervention as a control group to help evaluate the changes attributable to the training.

In addition, this research extended the work performed by O'Neill and Xiao (2004) by testing their hypothesis that identity theft training had the potential to increase the use of risk-reduction behaviors, by examining the effects of CASE. This research determined that the CASE model, tailored to the senior population, had a positive influence on changing both attitudes and behaviors of seniors with respect to the utilization of preventive strategies.

7.2 Implications for Future Research

Senior citizens have been identified as the primary victims of identity theft (Walters, 2004) and research suggests that consistent use of preventive techniques can have a significant impact on reducing the incidence of the crime. This dissertation research revealed the positive effects of the CASE training on the attitudes and behaviors of seniors with respect to identity theft prevention.

Further research is warranted to determine whether the CASE training has had continued or prolonged effects on the positive behavior changes that resulted. A longitudinal study of behaviors and attitudes of seniors with respect to identity theft prevention may lead to additional insights into the factors that influence the adoption of recommended techniques.

Furthermore, the analysis of the influence of demographic characteristics yielded results that warrant further investigation. Some demographic variables such as marital status, education and income may be predictors of adopting preventive behaviors as a training outcome and should be explored with larger samples to determine their impact on behavioral changes. Research into these factors may also provide insight on ways to improve training which is geared to specific demographic groups.

Another demographic factor explored in this study which warrants further investigation, is the influence of Internet access upon the attitudes and behaviors of seniors. This research seems to indicate that seniors without such access had lower response levels to the training. This phenomenon should be explored more fully to determine how the lack of Internet access influences seniors' perceptions of the threat of identity theft and how training programs can increase the identity theft awareness of this group.

While seniors have been the primary victims of identity theft, the crime has the potential to harm all citizens. Additional research into the applicability of the CASE training model to other age groups is further suggested by the researcher.

7.3 Implications for Practitioners

Identity theft victims of all ages have experienced the negative effects of this crime. It often takes months, or even years, to recover from being a victim (ITRC, 2003). Government agencies and organizations that serve as advocates for senior citizens need to take a move proactive role in protecting this segment of the citizenry (Milne, 2003).

Previous research has suggested that more identity theft training programs are needed (Milne, 2003; O'Neill & Xiao, 2004; Titus; 1999). As a result of the positive effects of the training found in this study, it is recommended that programs such as CASE be provided through a greater number and variety of venues, such as recreational centers, community centers, senior centers and places of worship. Offering training through organizations that seniors trust can provide the opportunity for greater positive behavior changes and increased awareness.

Continued awareness of the threat of identity theft and reminders of effective prevention techniques are important in maintaining behaviors that reduce victimization. Additional resources for training reinforcement need to be made available to seniors. Newsletters and fraud alerts such as those produced by CASE, need to be distributed and available to a greater audience. A variety of media, including DVDs, email and print, should be utilized to provide greater accessibility to training and reinforcement materials.

The results of this study will be shared with the CASE developers, leadership and trainers to assist them in evaluating and revising the established program. Specifically, the results with respect to the time devoted to specific topics and the related levels of change, will be discussed with the trainers to help them refine the curriculum to produce greater positive impacts and build on successful approaches.

In addition, continuous evaluation of the CASE program is recommended to assess its effectiveness in different settings to ensure that it continues to address gaps in identity theft awareness that exist among senior citizens.

7.4 Conclusions

Research has shown that seniors are among the most vulnerable targets of identity theft. This study examined the effect of the CASE training program on the attitudes and behaviors of seniors with respect to identity theft prevention and found that the senior-centric approach of the CASE training yielded positive changes. The findings of this research suggest that access to seniors through trusted communities, such as churches, increases the potential that this population can be educated about the threats that exist and the benefits of employing simple techniques in preventing this crime. Programs such as CASE have the potential to have a positive impact on the senior population by facilitating significant changes in their attitudes and behaviors with respect to identity theft prevention techniques, and ultimately reduce the incidence of identity theft experienced by this vulnerable group.

APPENDICES

Appendix A

List of Acronyms

AARP - American Association of Retired People

BBB- Better Business Bureau

CASE- Clergy Against Senior Exploitation

DAO- District Attorney's Office

FACTA- Fair and Accurate Credit Transactions

FTC- Federal Trade Commission

GECs- Geriatric Education Centers

ITRC- Identity Theft Resource Center

USPS– United States Postal Services

VA- Veteran's Administration

Appendix B

Instruments

Part 1 - Risk Assessment Pre-Treatment Survey

CASE Identity Theft Prevention Seminar Survey

Welcome to the *Clergy Against Senior Exploitation (CASE) Identity theft Prevention Seminar.*

In order to help us evaluate the CASE *Identity Theft Prevention Program*, please complete this survey.

Your responses are very important and will be kept strictly confidential. For security reasons, each survey is coded with an identification number that protects your identity. Only the researcher has access to the list that associates this number with you. The information collected in this survey will be published only in aggregate form.

If you have any questions, please ask the researcher for assistance. Your participation in this survey is sincerely appreciated. Thank you for attending.

Your Attitudes Towards Identity Theft Prevention

Item No.	Below are 10 statements about identity theft. Please indicate if you agree or disagree with each statement by selecting the appropriate number on the scale of 1 (Strongly Agree) to 5 (Not Applicable) that most closely matches your beliefs.	Strongly Agree	Moderately Agree	Moderately Disagree	Strongly Disagree	Not Applicable
1)	I should destroy old bank statements.	1	2	3	4	5
2)	I should destroy old credit card receipts.	1	2	3	4	5
3)	I should destroy unused pre-approved credit card offers.	1	2	3	4	5
4)	I should destroy old personal correspondence.	1	2	3	4	5
5)	I should destroy old pay stubs.	1	2	3	4	5
6)	I should destroy old utility bills.	1	2	3	4	5
7)	I should not reveal my social security number to telemarketers.	1	2	3	4	5
8)	I should place out-going mail in a secure mailbox.	1	2	3	4	5
9)	I should not give out my contact information to whoever asks for it.	1	2	3	4	5
10)	I should not carry my social security card in my wallet or purse.	1	2	3	4	5

Your Behavior Towards Identity Theft Prevention

Item No.	Below are 10 statements about identity theft. Please describe your behavior by selecting the appropriate number on the scale of 1 (Always) to 5 (Not Applicable) that most closely matches your current and past behavior.	Always	Occasionally	Rarely	Never	Not Applicable
1)	I destroy old bank statements.	1	2	3	4	5
2)	I destroy old credit card receipts.	1	2	3	4	5
3)	I destroy unused pre-approved credit card offers.	1	2	3	4	5
4)	I destroy old personal correspondence.	1	2	3	4	5
5)	I destroy old pay stubs.	1	2	3	4	5
6)	I destroy old utility bills.	1	2	3	4	5
7)	I do not reveal my social security number to telemarketers.	1	2	3	4	5
8)	I place out-going mail in a secure mailbox.	1	2	3	4	5
9)	I do not give out my contact information to whoever asks for it.	1	2	3	4	5
10)	I do not carry my social security card in my wallet or purse.	1	2	3	4	5

Demographic Information

For the following questions, please check the box that best applies.

What is your first language?
- ☐ English
- ☐ Other

What is your gender?
- ☐ Male
- ☐ Female

What is your current age?
- ☐ 49 or younger
- ☐ 50-64
- ☐ 65-74
- ☐ 75 and over

What is your work status?
- ☐ Working full-time
- ☐ Working part-time
- ☐ Retired
- ☐ Other

What is your race?
- ☐ Caucasian/White
- ☐ Hispanic/Latino
- ☐ African-American/Black
- ☐ Asian/Pacific Islander
- ☐ Native American
- ☐ Other

What is your current income level?
- ☐ Less than $25,000
- ☐ $25,000 to $49,000
- ☐ $50,000 to $99,000
- ☐ $100,000 and above

What is your marital status?
☐ Single
☐ Married
☐ Divorced
☐ Widowed

What is the highest educational level you have completed?
☐ High School Diploma/GED
☐ Bachelor's Degree
☐ Master's Degree
☐ PhD
☐ Other

Do you know what a credit report is?
☐ Yes
☐ No

Do you know how to order a credit report?
☐ Yes
☐ No

Have you ordered a credit report within the last 12 months?
☐ Yes
☐ No
☐ Not Sure

If you ordered a credit report, did someone assist you?
☐ Yes
☐ No

Do you have access to the Internet?
☐ Yes
☐ No

Thank you for taking the time to respond to this survey!

CASE Identity Theft Prevention Seminar Post Survey

Welcome to the *Clergy Against Senior Exploitation (CASE) Identity theft Prevention Seminar*. In order to help us evaluate the CASE *Identity Theft Prevention Program*, please complete this survey.

Your responses are very important and will be kept strictly confidential. For security reasons, each survey is coded with an identification number that protects your identity. Only the researcher has access to the list that associates this number with you. The information collected in this survey will be published only in aggregate form.

If you have any questions, please ask the researcher for assistance. Your participation in this survey is sincerely appreciated. Thank you for attending.

Your Attitudes Towards Identity Theft Prevention

Item No.	Below are 10 statements about identity theft. Please indicate if you agree or disagree with each statement by selecting the appropriate number on the scale of 1 (Strongly Agree) to 5 (Not Applicable) that most closely matches your beliefs.	Strongly Agree	Moderately Agree	Moderately Disagree	Strongly Disagree	Not Applicable
1)	I should destroy old bank statements.	1	2	3	4	5
2)	I should destroy old credit card receipts.	1	2	3	4	5
3)	I should destroy unused pre-approved credit card offers.	1	2	3	4	5
4)	I should destroy old personal correspondence.	1	2	3	4	5
5)	I should destroy old pay stubs.	1	2	3	4	5
6)	I should destroy old utility bills.	1	2	3	4	5
7)	I should reveal my social security number to telemarketers.	1	2	3	4	5
8)	I should place out-going mail in a secure mailbox.	1	2	3	4	5
9)	I should give out my contact information to whoever asks for it.	1	2	3	4	5
10)	I should carry my social security card in my wallet or purse.	1	2	3	4	5

Your Behavior Towards Identity Theft Prevention

Item No.	Below are 10 statements about identity theft. Please describe your behavior by selecting the appropriate number on the scale of 1 (Always) to 5 (Not Applicable) that most closely matches your current and past behavior.	Always	Occasionally	Rarely	Never	Not Applicable
1)	I destroy old bank statements.	1	2	3	4	5
2)	I destroy old credit card receipts.	1	2	3	4	5
3)	I destroy unused pre-approved credit card offers.	1	2	3	4	5
4)	I destroy old personal correspondence.	1	2	3	4	5
5)	I destroy old pay stubs.	1	2	3	4	5
6)	I destroy old utility bills.	1	2	3	4	5
7)	I reveal my social security number to telemarketers.	1	2	3	4	5
8)	I place out-going mail in a secure mailbox.	1	2	3	4	5
9)	I give out my contact information to whoever asks for it.	1	2	3	4	5
10)	I carry my social security card in my wallet or purse.	1	2	3	4	5

1) In the past two weeks, have you ordered a credit report? If so, what made you order the report?

2) What form of identity theft do you think I the worst and why?

3) Are you less concerned about identity theft today than you were two weeks ago?

4) Do you carry your social security card with you and why?

5) Does your spouse worry more about identity theft than you do? Are most of your bills in your spouse's name?

6) To what extent has the Veteran's Administration computer theft affected your attitudes and behavior?

_____

Thank you for taking the time to respond to this survey!

Appendix C

Letter to Dr O'Neill

From: Lorenza Whitfield [mailto:lo_dog98@yahoo.com]

Sent: Tuesday, October 18, 2005 7:54 PM

To: oneill@aesop.rutgers.edu

Subject: Identity theft Result Risk Quiz and White Paper

Hello Dr. O'Neill,

This is Lorenza Whitfield. It was a pleasure talking with you tonight on identity theft. I am a student at the University of Fairfax working on my PH D. As you know, identity theft crime is growing everyday. There are preventative techniques but they are not being followed because the crime is still growing daily. I am doing my dissertation concerning attitudes about identity theft. The Identity theft Risk Assessment Quiz that Dr. Xiao and you made on measuring whether people are employing these risk reduction techniques is perfect for my research.

Per our conversation, could you please email me your full paper called, "Consumer Practices to Reduce Identity theft Risk: An Exploratory Study"? Also, I would like your permission to use your quiz the same way you did when you conducted your experiment online.

Thanks for talking to me tonight and I am sorry for interrupting your dinner. I will call you tomorrow.

Sincerely,

Lorenza Whitfield

(703) 613-2849 (Work)

(703) 729-5204 (Home)

Appendix D

Letter from Dr O'Neill

Wed, 19 Oct 2005 09:24:55 -0400

From: "Barbara O'Neill" <oneill@AESOP.Rutgers.edu>

Subject: Paper

To: lo_do898@yahoo.com

Lorenza:

You have my permission to link to our online Identity theft Risk Assessment

Quiz. Attached is the file for my paper and some other resources.

Barbara O'Neill, Ph.D., CFP, CRPC, AFC, CHC, CFCS

Extension Specialist in Financial Resource Management

Professor II

Rutgers Cooperative Research and Extension

Cook College Office Building Room 107

55 Dudley Road

New Brunswick, NJ 08901

Phone: 732-932-9155 Extension 250

Phone: 973-903-7869 (cell)

Fax: 732-932-8887

E-mail: oneill@aesop.rutgers.edu

Internet: http://www.rce.rutgers.edu/money2000

   http://www.investing.rutgers.edu

Letter to CASE

-----Original Message-----
From: Lorenza Whitfield [mailto:*lwhitfield@students.ufairfax.net*]
Sent: Friday, February 17, 2006 10:02 AM
To: Lisa Curtis
Cc: *jorcutt@ufairfax.net*
Subject:

Dear Mrs. Curtis,

This email is a follow up to a phone call you had with Janice Orcutt, Dean of Academic Affairs with the University of Fairfax, located in Vienna, Virginia. I am a doctoral candidate in the field of Information Assurance Policy at the University of Fairfax and am investigating the impact of training in changing senior citizen behavior in the area of identity theft prevention. Given that older Americans are increasingly targeted as victims in this type of crime, I am very interested in finding validated training methods for the senior population for use in my research.

I found a reference to your program (CASE) on the Internet which prompted the call from the Dean. From the description on your website it appears that at least a portion of the training that is conducted could meet the requirements for my dissertation research. Given that your program has an established approach to educating seniors, I would like to explore the possibility of working with one of your partner organizations in the greater Washington DC area in order to complete my research. I believe my research will be complementary to the goals of your program.

Specifically, my dissertation research intends to:

1) Assess the attitudes of seniors toward the use of the identity theft prevention techniques, such as ordering a credit report, prior to training and
2) Investigate whether seniors exposed to training will demonstrate a behavior change with respect to the use of these prevention techniques, and
3) Determine the primary influencing factor in the behavior change that is observed.

I have contacted three senior housing complexes (independent living for seniors) in Loudoun County, Virginia about my research and all three are receptive (and anxious) for this type of training for their residents. Participation in the study will be voluntary and not required for participation in the training.

Ideally if you have an affiliate in Loudoun County, I would appreciate you providing me contact information, but I am more than willing to work with any established affiliate in the greater DC area. I can be contacted at this email address (*lwhitfield@students.ufairfax.net*) or via phone at 703-622-5871. Alternatively, your affiliate can contact the Dean, Janice Orcutt, at the University (703-790-3200 x105) or via email at *jorcutt@ufairfax.net*.

I look forward to a positive response from your organization and will be happy to share the results of my study and the completed dissertation with you.

Sincerely,

Lorenza A. Whitfield
43475 Plantation Terrace
Ashburn, VA 20147

Letter from CASE

To: "Lorenza Whitfield" <lwhitfield@students.ufairfax.net>
Date: Tue, 21 Feb 2006 14:32:51 -0700
From: "Lisa Curtis" <*Llc@denverda.org*>
Subject: RE:

Mr. Whitfield,

We are contacting the Loudoun County DA's Office about being the trainer for your programs. Our CASE Model Site contact at the Annapolis State's Attorney Office has committed to helping the Loudoun County DA receive the training and info needed to use our CASE fraud prevention materials.

We will confirm our plans in the next few days.

Lisa Curtis

Director, Consumer Services

Denver District Attorney's Office

201 W. Colfax, Dept. 801

Denver, CO 80202

LLC@denverda.org

720-913-9178

720-913-9177 FAX

Sample Fraud Alert

FRAUD ALERT!

FRAUD ALERT!

From Anne Arundel County State's Attorney

Frank Weathersbee's Office

Your Free Credit Report – Get It!

Everyone in the US is entitled to get free copies of their credit reports from the three major credit bureaus each year. Getting your credit report is as important a guard against ID theft as is checking your account statements.

But use caution when getting your free credit report as some websites and telemarketers are tricking people into paying. Never respond to an e-mail or telephone offer for a free credit report - you may be linked to a bogus site or a crook trying to steal Social Security Numbers. Don't search for the web site by typing in "Free Credit Report" - you may get a site where you'll be baited with a free report but have to buy credit report monitoring or a credit score. If you're asked for your credit card number, it's not free!

www.annualcreditreport.com is the ONLY authorized online source to get a free credit report under federal law. **www.annualcreditreport.com** is secure, easy to use and free. You can also get your free credit report by telephone by calling 877-322-8228.

On-line: www.annualcreditreport.com
Phone: 1-877-322-8228
Mail: Annual Credit Report Service
        P.O.   Box   105281
        Atlanta, GA 30348-5281

Anne Arundel SA's Fraud Line:
410.222.1740 ext. 3845

CASE is a Partnership of the State's Attorney
and the Community to Prevent Elder Financial
Exploitation

Appendix H

Detailed Schedule of Events

Day 1- May 17, 2006:

Pre-Treatment survey, Treatment Group: St. Philip's Episcopal Church

- 11:30 AM- Researcher met with the St. Philip's Episcopal Church's leadership to ask and answer questions.

- 12:00 Noon- Participants were greeted by a high-profile identity theft professional, Kristin Riggins, and Anne Arundel County State's Attorney, Frank Weatherbee. Kristin Riggins conducted the CASE training.

- 12:15 P.M. - The researcher was introduced by Ms. Riggins, and researcher asked participants to complete pre-treatment surveys.

- 12:30 P.M.-CASE training began; the researcher remained as an observer.

- The researcher informed the participants of a follow-up visit that would take place in two weeks on 5/31/2006 at 12:00P.M.

- The researcher ensured that the Maryland DA's office send out the fraud alert that was in Appendix F.

Pre-Treatment Survey, Comparison Group: Wingler House

- 7:00 PM- Researcher met with the volunteer participants in the chapel at the Wingler House.

- 7:05 PM: Researcher distributed the surveys.

- 7:25 PM: Researcher collected the surveys.

- The researcher informed the participants that a follow-up visit would take place on 5/31/2006 at 7:00 PM.

Day 2- May 31, 2006:

Post- Treatment Survey, Treatment Group: St. Philip's Episcopal Church

- 11:45P.M. - Refreshments

- 12:00 Noon - The participants were asked to complete the post-treatment survey.

- Interviews Conducted

Comparison Group: Wingler House

- 6:45- Refreshments

- 7:00- Participants were asked to complete the post-treatment survey.

- Interviews Conducted

Day 3- Second Session Pre-Treatment survey

June 20, 2006:

Pre-Treatment survey, Treatment Group: Heritage Baptist Church

- 11:30 AM- Researcher met with the St. Philips Episcopal Church's leadership to ask and answer questions.

- 12:00 Noon- Participants were greeted by a high-profile identity theft professional, Kristin Riggins, and Anne Arundel County State's Attorney, Frank Weatherbee. Kristin Riggins conducted the CASE training.

- 12:15 P.M. - The researcher was introduced by Ms. Riggins, and participants were asked by the researcher to complete the pre-treatment surveys.

- 12:30 P.M.- CASE training began; the researcher remained as an observer.

June 18, 2006

Pre-Treatment survey, Comparison Group: Mt. Pleasant Baptist Church

- 1:00 PM- Researcher met with the volunteer participants in the chapel of the Mt. Pleasant Baptist Church.

- 1:10 PM: Researcher distributed the surveys.

- 1:30 PM: Researcher collected the surveys.

- The researcher informed the participants that a follow-up visit would take place on 7/9/2006, following church services.

Day 4- Second Session Post-Treatment Survey

July 5, 2006:

Post-Treatment Survey: Treatment Group: Heritage Baptist Church

- 11:45P.M. - Refreshments 12:00P.M. - The participants were asked to complete the post-treatment survey.

- Interviews conducted

July 9, 2006:

Post Survey: Comparison Group: Mt. Pleasant Baptist Church

- 1:00- The participants were asked to complete the post-treatment survey.

- Interviews conducted

Reference List

ABC7Chicago.com. (2005) *DSW identity theft worse than first believed.* Retrieved May 28 2006, from http://abclocal.go.com/wls/story?section=News&id=2984721

Allison, S.F., Schuck, A. M., & Lersch, K.M. (2005). Exploring the crime of identity theft: Prevalence, clearance rates, and victim/offender characteristics. *Journal of Criminal Justice, 33*, 19-29.

American Association of Retired Persons. (1996). *Telemarketing fraud and older Americans: An AARP study.* Conducted by Princeton Survey Research Associates.

American Association of Retired Persons. (1997). *Comparative findings from the 1996 & 1997 Omnibus surveys on telemarketing fraud.* Prepared by the Evaluation Research Services, Research Division, June.

American Association of Retired People (2006). Preventing Identity Theft: Retrieved May 26, 2006, from http://www.aarp.org/learntech/personal_finance/identity_theft_intro.html

Benner, J., Givens, B. & Mierzwinski, E. (2000). Nowhere to Turn: Victims speak out on identity theft: A CALPIRG/ Privacy Rights Clearinghouse report. *Privacy Rights Clearinghouse.* Retrieved July 18, 2005, from http://www.privacyrights.org/ar/idtheft2000.htm

Better Business Bureau (2006). *Online Shopping Tips.* Retrieved January 15, 2006, from http://www.bbbonline.org/IDTheft/

CALPIRG (2000). Nowhere to turn: Victims speak out on identity theft. *A CALPIRG/Privacy Right Clearinghouse Report,* May 2000. Sacramento, Calif.: Privacy Rights Clearinghouse.

DSW (2005). *Press Release.* Retrieved May 28, 2006, from http://www.dswshoe.com/credit_card_faq.jsp

Edwards, S. (2003). *House Committee on Ways and Means.* Retrieved April 14, 2006, from http://waysandmeans.house.gov/hearings.asp?formmode=view&id=658#_edn2

Federal Trade Commission. (2000). *When bad things happen to your good name*. Retrieved September 19, 2005, from http://www.ftc.gov/bcp/conline/pubs/credit/idtheft.htm

Federal Trade Commission. (2003a). *Commission and Staff Reports Identity Theft Report*. Retrieved November 9, 2005, from http://www.ftc.gov/reports/index.thm

Federal Trade Commission. (2003b) *Identity theft Survey Report*. Washington, DC: U.S. Government Printing Office.

Federal Trade Commission (2004a). *Identity theft victim complaint data: figures and trends on identity theft for AARP January 1-December 31, 2003*. (March 2004).

Federal Trade Commission. (2004b). *National and state trends in fraud and identity theft January - December 2003*. Retrieved August 6,2005, from http://www.consumer.gov/sentinel/pubs/Top10Fraud2003.pdf

Federal Trade Commission (2005a). *Take charge: Fighting back against identity theft –* June 2005. Retrieved August 6, 2005, from www.ftc.gov/bcp/conline/pubs/credit/idtheft.htm

Federal Trade Commission. (2005b). *Nation and State Trends in Fraud and Identity theft January* December 2004. Retrieved August 6, 2005 from http://www.consumer.gov/sentinel/pubs/Top10Fraud2004.pdf

Federal Trade Commission. (2006a). *Nation and State Trends in Fraud and Identity theft January* December 2005. Retrieved March 18, 2006, from http://www.consumer.gov/sentinel/pubs/Top10Fraud2005.pdf

Federal Trade Commission. (2006b). *Welcome to federal trade commission- Your national resource against identity theft*. Retrieved March 23, 2006, from http://www.consumer.gov/idtheft/

FirstGov.gov. (2006). Latest information on Veterans Affairs data security. Retrieved May 18, 2006, from http: www.firstgov.gov/veteransinfo.shtml

Glatthorn, A.A. (1994) Constructivism: Implications for Curriculum. International. *Journal of Education Reforms, 3*(4), 449 – 455.

Identity Theft Resource Center. (2003). *Facts and statistics*. Retrieved July 2, 2002, from http://www.idtheftcenter.org/facts.shtml.

Identity Theft Resource Center. (2005). Other PRC identity theft publications, speeches, and testimony. Retrieved August 6, 2005, from http://idtheftcenter.org/index.shtml.

International Association of Chiefs of Police. (2000). *Curbing Identity theft*

Resolutions. Retrieved June 12, 2005, from
http://www.theiacp.org/Resolutions/index.cfm?fuseaction=dis_public_view&resolution_id=20&CFID=138190&CFTOKE=34557922

Javelin/Better Business Bureau, *2005. Identity Fraud Survey Report* 2005. Retrieved December 13, 2005, from
http://www.javelinstrategy.com/reports/2005IdentityFraudSurveyReport.html

Karia, N., & Asari, M.H.A.H. (2001). *Identity theft: What can we learn?* Retrieved January 2, 2006, from http://mhasmi.tripod.com/paper/idtheft-dm2002.pdf

Lease, M., & Burke,T. (2000). Identity theft: A fast growing crime. *FBI Law Enforcement Bulletin, 69*(8), 8.

Kloos, B., & Moore, T. (2000). The prospect and purpose of locating community research and action in religious setting. *Journal of Community Psychology, 28*(2), 119-137.

Malks, B., Schmidt C., & Austin, M. (2002). Prevention: A case study of the Santa Clara county financial abuse specialist team (FAST) program. *Journal of Gerontological Social Work. 39*(3), 23-40.

McConnell C. F., Dwyer, W. O., & Leening, F. C. (1996). A behavioral approach to reducing fires in public housing, *Journal of Community Psychology (24)*2, 201-212.

McKenna, J. & Miller, J. (2003). *An evaluation of the clergy against senior exploitation (CASE) fraud prevention education program.* Retrieved February 20, 2006, from Colorado State University, Family Economics Extension Specialist site: http://www.ext.colostate.edu/staffres/case.pdf

Milne, G. R. (2003). How well do consumers protect themselves from identity theft? *Journal of Consumer Affairs, 37*(2), 288-402.

Moore, E., & Mills, M. (1990) The neglected victims and unexamined cost of white collar crime. *Crime & Delinquency (36),* 408-418.

Morrissey, M.R., & Curtis, L. (2005). Partnering with faith communities to prevent elder fraud and exploitation. *The Prosecuter*, 10-47.

O'Neill, B. (2003). Give your clients (and yourself!) an identity theft risk assessment. *Journal of Personal Finance, 2*(2), 26-38.

O'Neill, B. & Xiao, J. (2004). Consumer practices to reduce identity theft: an exploratory study, *Consumer Interests Annual, 50,* 125-127.

Parlak, B.A., & Klein, S.M. (1997). Geriatric education center: Preparing the healthy workforce to serve an aging nation. *Generation, 20,* 78-81.

Privacy Rights Clearinghouse. (2003). *Identity theft IQ test.* Washington, DC: Retrieved November 18, 2005 from www.privacyrights.org/itrc-quiz1.htm

S. Rep. No. 105-274 (1998). Identity theft and assumption deterrence act: Amendment of federal sentencing guidelines for offenses under section 1028. Washington, DC: Retrieved May 28, 2006 from http://www.ftc.gov/os/statutes/itada/itadact.htm#004

S. Rep. No. 108-159 (2003). The Fair and Accurate Credit Transactions Act (FACTA). Washington, DC: Retrieved May 28, 2006 from http://www.privacyrights.org/fs/fs6a-facta.htm

Stein, J. (1999). Changing attitudes about substance abuse: A study to assess the impact of a training program for social work students. *Dissertation Abstract International, II*(ii). (UMI No. 9941697)

Titus, R. (1999). *The victimology of fraud.* Washington, DC:U. S. National Institute of Justice.

Titus, R. M., Heinzelmann, F., & Boyle, J. (1995). Victimization of persons by fraud. *Crime & Delinquency, 41*(1), 54-72.

U.S. Postal Service. (2005). *Identity theft is the fastest growing crime.* Retrieved May 7, 2005, from http://www.usps.com/postalinspectors/idthft_ncpw.htm

U.S. Securities and Exchange Commission. (2006). *Protecting Seniors Strategy.* Washington, DC: Retrieved August 14, 2006 from http://www.sec.gov/news/press/extra/seniors/protectingseniors.htm

Walters, N. (2004). Identity theft: An update on the experience of older complainants. *Public Policy Institute Data Digest, 102.* Retrieved November 11, 2005 from http://www.aarp.org/research/frauds-scams/fraud/aresearch-import-919-DD102.html

Walters, N. & Jackson, A. (2003). Identity theft: Experience of older complainants. *Public Policy Institute Data Digest, 85.* Retrieved November 11, 2005, from http://research.aarp.org/consume/dd85_idtheft.html

Winge, E. (2003). Effectives of a smoking simulation on students' smoking attitudes. *American Journal of Health Studies, 18*, 2-3.

Wright, S., Caserta, M. & Lund, D. (2003). Older adults' attitudes, concerns, and support for environmental issues in the "New West". *International Journal on Aging and Human Development*, 57(2), 151-179.

Biography

Lorenza A. Whitfield currently serves as the lead Enterprise Information Management Architect for the Enterprise Engineering Center at Lockheed Martin Corporation where he directs the design and installation of management information systems for Fortune 1000 corporations.

Previously, he held positions of increasing responsibility in all facets of network engineering and information systems with several organizations, including Vitro Corporation, Lucent Technologies and DynCorp Systems Solutions.

Lorenza earned his BS in Electronic Engineering Technology from Virginia State University and his MLS in Information Security from Eastern Michigan University. In addition, he holds numerous Cisco certifications as well as the Best Practices Certification from the IT Information Library Foundation.

Printed in the United States
by Baker & Taylor Publisher Services